CW01332951

Align Your Life

Get Out of Your Own Way and
Create a Life You Love.

By Kim Ryder

Copyright © 2021 Kim Ryder

All rights reserved. Published by Kim Ryder, Total Integrated Therapy LLC. Printed in the USA.

No part of this publication may be reproduced, shared, photocopied, recorded, or used in any other way without written permission of the author Kim Ryder. For information regarding permission, write to;

Kim Ryder at Total Integrated Therapy,
info@totalintegratedtherapy.com.

ISBN: 978-1-63760-818-0

Dedication

I dedicate this book to the people of the world,
my beautiful family, and friends who have
supported, encouraged and helped me throughout
my life's journey. Thank you for
all your love and blessings.

Also, by Kim Ryder and Dave Ryder

Activate Your Unique Purpose Course: This is a powerful step-by-step transformational modulated program to develop and activate your meaningful purpose.

I Can Change the Way I Feel – Tap Away Your Troubles: This is a tapping book for children to learn how to tap and overcome stressful situations or difficulties.

Magnetic Money Mindsets: Automatically train your mind to create a magnetic money mindset for growth, prosperity, and financial abundance.

Attracting Loving Relationships: Automatically program your mind to attract new opportunities and loving relationships into your life.

Maximum Health and Wellness: Automatically program your mind to create a healthier internal environment for your body to thrive.

All the above available by visiting:
https://www.breakthroughmindsets.com

Supporting Material to Create a Life You Love

Our website has free health and wellness resources to support your journey to empowerment. Here you will find special audio recordings and videos, plus other inspirational programs and courses to support your personal growth and continued learning.

https://www.totalintegratedtherapy.com/resources-for-health-and-wellness/

For other video resources, head to our YouTube channel "Breakthrough Mindsets"

https://www.youtube.com/breakthroughmindsets/

Contents

ACKNOWLEDGMENT **8**

INTRODUCTION **9**

INSPIRATIONAL JOURNAL **12**

CHAPTER 1 AUTHENTIC CONNECTIONS **14**

CHAPTER 2 ALIGN YOUR MIND-BODY **36**

CHAPTER 3 ALIGN WITH FOCUS AND CLARITY **53**

CHAPTER 4 INSPIRED ACTION **64**

CHAPTER 5 MINDFUL AWARENESS **83**

CHAPTER 6 LIFE BY DESIGN **100**

CHAPTER 7 MAKING CHANGES **113**

Acknowledgment

I want to share my heartfelt gratitude to my amazing husband, Dave Ryder, who has helped me beyond measure to bring structure to my ideas. Special thanks to Joyce Ryder for her tireless editing, refining, and helping me to complete another book.

All those who came before me and crossed my path, who have shared their insights, wisdom, and knowledge. To all my teachers, past and present, you helped me grow into the human being I have become. With heartfelt love, gratitude, and appreciation, I acknowledge you all for your contributions to the world.

Thank you.

Introduction

The book you are reading arose from my love of teaching and helping people consciously align with their true self, and a meaningful purpose. For many years I've been helping people to get out of their own way, so they can align their life with what they truly want. Many of these people struggled with limiting beliefs and one-sided perceptions, therefore, blocking themselves from creating happy, peaceful, and purposeful states of mind.

Align Your Life was written to help people be more effective in creating a loving, joyous, peaceful, and fulfilling life. This book has evolved into a truly meaningful guide that integrates new concepts, processes, and practical tools that can be applied to help people of all ages. If you have been seeking a way to consciously self-direct your life in a way you are truly meant to live, your search is over.

Aligning your life means to connect with your authentic self and principle powers that will guide you in the direction of what is truly important to you. You will learn how to connect with your true self at a deep level, clearly refine what you truly want, reveal the secret power of why, define your goals and realize them.

You will be given the tools and techniques to identify and overcome the obstacles and challenges in your path to attaining your desired goals. You'll learn how to release the emotional roadblocks that distract you from what you want to accomplish. These include past regrets, guilts, resentments, fear of failure, grief, loss, and other stressful limiting emotions. You will be empowered to overcome these obstacles and align your life the way you really want it to be.

Throughout *Align Your Life,* there are powerful insights and effective processes to explore. You will gain understanding about doing what you love and inspiration for living life with purpose and meaning. Furthermore, in breaking through your fears, confusion, and distractions, you can become clear about what you would love to contribute and dedicate your life to. You will learn empowering affirmations that, when practiced consistently, will begin to change your mind for success. This will build your confidence and clarity and align your thoughts, words, and actions with what you want to create.

I believe we are all born with a divine purpose, and when we align our lives with that purpose, we can accomplish extraordinary things and live exceptional lives. Your unique purpose is fuel for your life. It is your gateway to fulfillment that aligns the universe to unfold in miraculous ways so that new opportunities appear and new doors open as if by magic. One thing for certain, we all have to travel our own path to wisdom.

Magic happens when you align your thoughts, feelings, and actions with your true self, unique values, and purpose. The healing methods in this book stem from the idea that everything you need to heal is already within you, blocked only by your own self-imposed limits. You are about to learn how to remove those limits.

This book is a guide to help you connect with your magnificent self, unique gifts, qualities, and abilities. My intention is to help you master the art of getting out of your own way, so you can align yourself with what you want to create in your life. We are creating a vibrational alignment with what you truly want.

You are going to learn a lot of great things about yourself. Make sure to do the exercises and activities that create a personal experience and understanding. You are going to be delighted with what you are about to develop in yourself. Congratulations on taking this step to aligning yourself with the life you love and deserve.

Love, light, and peace
Kim

Inspirational Journal

Your Inspirational Journal or notebook will be a great additional support while reading this book. Start it as soon as you can and use it as you work through this book.

Starting your Inspirational Journal – Start with a blank notebook and write down all your answers to the questions I give you throughout this book. You can also write down inspirational ideas, daily gratitude and add photos or drawings.

Journals are a great way to measure your goals and also what you have accomplished. It's fun to include all your good experiences, happy memories, and as a reminder of your ideas and inspirational moments. Journaling is about creating a meaningful connection with yourself while recording thoughts and feelings. There are no rules although most journaling is a daily exercise.

At the back of your Inspirational Journal, you can add any challenging feelings, emotions, memories, experiences, and issues, so you can address them and make peace with them. Use the breakthrough tapping process to address these issues in chapter 7.

Make your Inspiration Journal personal and unique.

12

Chapter 1
Authentic Connections

Activate a State of Self-Awareness
Self-Love
Self-Love Exercise
Self- Acceptance
Self-Appreciation
The Gratitude Power Practice
Kindness
Self-Care
Crafting the State of Self-Love
Affirmations

Our Connections and Relationships
Support and Challenge
Inspirational Connections
Loving Connections
Strategies for Dealing with Difficult Relationships
Affirmations

Inner Knowing
Trust Yourself and your Abilities
Awareness
Seeing Both Sides
Reset Yourself
Affirmations
Powerful Self-Love Habits
Self-Love Habits Exercise
Affirmations

Chapter 1
Authentic Connections

"The privilege of a lifetime is to become who you truly are." - C.G. Jung

Activate a State of Self-Awareness

You are the single most important person in your world, and you have the most impact and influence on your life. It is beneficial to realize that everything in your life flows from the quality of your relationship with yourself. Your essence relates to an awareness of your intrinsic nature and your unique qualities. Allowing yourself to express your essence, the core of who you really are empowers personal growth.

People that don't understand how valuable and important they are tend to get stuck operating from conditioned behaviors, beliefs, and an old identity that dictates the outcome and results they get in their life. In other words, they live from a version of reality that limits their potential. This results in living a life of fantasy and illusion. By having this self-awareness of your true nature, you create a state of being conscious of your own individuality, feelings, emotions, motives, and desires.

Self-Love

Loving yourself is at the heart of experiencing authentic connections. Not everybody was taught how to love themselves growing up. It's hard when you don't have a self-loving role model.

I personally had to learn how to lovingly connect with myself, and it took many years to do it. There were decades of family conditioning and beliefs that had large cables attached that I needed to break free from. I had to unlearn the constant seeking for love and approval outside of myself and let go of feelings of not good enough. My search for unconditional love was over when I realized everything I needed in the way of love was inside of me already. The love was already there, and I realized that I am full of love, and you have everything you need inside of you too.

The beginning of my self-love journey was when I started a consistent practice of yoga and meditation. During this time, I integrated many other healing methods to support the flow of self-love. I'm going to show you how quick and easy it is to lovingly connect to your authentic self. The rewards of self-love are many.

Self-Love Exercise

Right now, close your eyes and connect to your heart and ask yourself, "What do I need?", and "How can I be more loving to myself"? Write your answers down in your inspirational journal.

Self-love is loving every part of yourself unconditionally, warts and all, every wrinkle, as well as the flabby bits. But it's not easy at first. There may be times when it feels impossible, especially if you have a negative self-image that needs to change.

When you look at yourself in the mirror and only see and say negative things, you are talking directly to your subconscious mind, which is sending messages to your body, conditioning your central nervous system and your body to react and respond accordingly. What you think about, you bring about! That's how you condition your mind. Your subconscious mind is a storehouse for the experiences you don't want or try to avoid. By changing what you express about yourself, you change the way you communicate and treat yourself.

Self-Acceptance

Self-acceptance is accepting all that you are right now and being at peace with all aspects of your being. This means to accept who you are and not who you think you are supposed to be. When you are self-accepting, you accept all aspects of yourself, both positive and negative. If you do not love or accept yourself, then you will seek love and acceptance outside of yourself instead of connecting to your true source of fulfilling love from within. This state of being "in love" is different from seeking or trying to find it. If you are not being "in love," you will never find enough love outside of yourself. You already have a never-ending source of love inside of you. This empowering mindset of knowing without a shadow of a doubt who you are, and what you already have inside is an abundance of love. Rather than seeking love, you are love. This understanding is one of the keys to your own personal development, success, and fulfillment.

When you don't know what's possible, who you are, where you are going, and your big why, then you live a reactionary unfulfilled existence. When you're coming from a mindset of knowing, then you perceive your roadblocks as just challenges from which you will grow and develop your natural qualities, gifts, and abilities. In times of challenge, having a self-loving spirit becomes an asset that can transform challenges into opportunities for growth. You get to choose how you want to respond and take charge with positive action.

It's only your daily conditioning and habits of mind that can keep you from moving forward. You may know someone who has faced the most inconceivable misfortune and somehow came out the other side stronger and more resilient. Personal growth and self-transformation occur as a result of these periods of challenge. Supporting yourself in a loving way is the balance you need while you are being challenged. This loving support will help you through even the most difficult of challenges.

Unfortunately, many cannot see past their own conditioned reactive minds. When we act in the opposite way, as opposed to loving, accepting, and understanding, we become our own worst critic, judge, and jury working against ourselves and our own potential.

How you see yourself and what you believe about yourself determines if you accept or reject yourself. It's important to be aware that before you can really love and accept another person, you must learn to love and accept yourself first. Self-acceptance is essential for your overall health and wellbeing. These attributes of love and self-acceptance affect not only your mental and emotional health, but also your physical health in very real and tangible ways.

The body is always listening for directions and responds to what you think, say, and believe. Loving and accepting yourself changes your perception of the world. It also changes your personal beliefs about who you think you are. Changing your perceptions about yourself can be challenging, especially if you are in the habit of looking outside yourself for love, acceptance, and approval. Love, acceptance, and approval are never enough to meet your needs when they come from outside. They are an inside job. When you love and accept yourself unconditionally, you are naturally motivated to take good care of yourself. Your decisions and goals will align with what is in your best interest and what is meaningful and fulfilling.

"Being in a state of self-awareness and self-love means accepting and validating every part of yourself despite of any changes you want to make."- *Kim Ryder*

Getting out of your own way and being your own best friend is something you learn and develop. When you learn to treat yourself like someone worthy of love, respect, and compassion, your life will express and attract more love, respect, and compassion. Life will begin to flow more effortlessly, abundantly, and more joyfully than you can imagine. Being in a state of self-love is the foundation for a life of success. This mindset shift that will help you become loving to the most important person in your life, you!

Self-Appreciation

Self-appreciation is gratitude of the highest order. When you appreciate yourself, your natural talents, and unique gifts, you can fulfill your heart's desire. For many years I had no appreciation for myself or what I had in my life. I felt disconnected and lost in the thoughts of what was missing instead of seeing what I had. I didn't realize that I had an abundance of life, love, and unique abilities. You can always appreciate where you are right now. You are here now with a wealth of knowledge, skills, and abilities. It's time to express them!

The Gratitude Power Practice

Use your inspirational journal to complete these 2 tasks.

1. *Write down 50 ways that you are grateful for being you. Expand this over time, and review this list to bring about a state of gratitude and appreciation of being you.*

2. *Every day, as part of your daily gratitude practice. Write down 3 things you are grateful for-review weekly.*

Gratitude is a powerful healing tool, as you are focused on what you are grateful for, it changes the expression of your gene cells and the cellular messages in your body. When you express gratitude, it is changing the vibration and the chemistry in you. This will help you to create a healthy state of mind and body, keeping the healthy gene cells switched on, and the unhealthy gene cells switched off. "Gratitude is a healing attitude!"

Kindness

Kindness is the skill of understanding and being gentle with yourself. It is showing yourself the greatest consideration and compassion. Before I learned how to be kind to myself, it was easy for me to berate and put myself down. I could be so mean, critical, and judgmental about myself. This did nothing for my self-confidence and stunted my personal growth and life experiences. Kindness began in the stillness of meditation. I learned to connect deeply with myself and to the divine source. For me, that became the most empowering practice and a gateway to unifying myself. Practice being kind to yourself. Repeat the affirmations at the end of this chapter. Feel the effects in your body and believe them in your heart and soul. Continue with the gratitude practice and read the list you have written about why you are grateful for being you.

Self-Care

Caring is the act of thoughtful affection. Caring for oneself is like cherishing a precious diamond that is irreplaceable. Caring for yourself is a valuable gift, it's being present and taking time out for your precious self. Connect with what is most meaningful and empowering to you. Do things you love to do, the things that make your heart sing, the things that make you laugh, smile, and give you a deep sense of peace.

Crafting the State of Self-Love

Do at least one thing every day that connects you to joy, such as moving, dancing, walking in the sun, or soaking in the bathtub. Happiness and joy are what you create on the inside and that comes from what you love and enjoy doing. It doesn't matter what you do, as long as it brings you joy. It's important that you take the time to do it. Block out a little time every day, because your happiness matters!

"I grasped the meaning of the greatest secret that human poetry and human thought and belief have to impart: The salvation of man is through love and in love." - Victor Frankl

Affirmations for Self-Awareness

Everything I need in the way of love is inside me, and I am full of love.
Gratitude flows within me, and around me, my life is abundant.
Kindness begins in the stillness of connecting to me and the divine.
I give myself the time I need to express the joy in my heart.
Caring for myself is valuing me in the highest order.

Our Connections and Relationships

"Our minds influence the key activity of the brain, which then influences everything; perception, cognition, thoughts and feelings, personal relationships; they're all a projection of you." - Deepak Chopra

Our relationships with people and things start from the day we are born. How we connect with ourselves and others takes shape from our relationships with the adults in our early years. They helped to shape our identity. Without knowing, we were being programmed and conditioned with their beliefs, behaviors, and perceptions of the world and life. How we love, nurture, and care for ourselves is learned from how the adults loved, nurtured, and cared for us as young children. Much of what we believe now comes from this early education. All of our relationships, whether from the food we eat, the car we drive, our home environment, or the people we spend time with, reflect how we feel about ourselves.

Our connections and relationships with others develop out of kindness or cruelty. These connections depend on how people see and feel about themselves.

When you hang around people that leave you feeling irritated, nervous, upset, guarded, tense, or uncomfortable in any way, you may wonder where those feelings come from. Very often, some part of what you are seeing is a reflection of a hidden belief you have about yourself, or it could be a belief about yourself that you are uneasy with. What someone else is doing or saying may trigger those hidden fears and insecurities. You may feel uncomfortable around them. Other people mirror what we secretly feel inside.

When you surround yourself with people who encourage you to feel loved and valued, part of what you feel reflects of your own belief that you deserve to be loved and appreciated. When you consciously choose the people who love and value themselves in your life, you are reinforcing and empowering those beliefs that you have about yourself.

Support and Challenge

Support and challenge are the foundation for growth. Too much support can hinder your growth and independence from thinking and making choices for yourself. Unrealistic challenges can have the opposite effect. As you become so self-reliant, you will find it difficult to allow others to support you. Equal amounts of support and challenge are the keys to balance. With this balance, it becomes easier to allow others to support you to flourish, and it also challenges you to be your best. It is also equally important to support and challenge yourself with a balanced perspective. By having support and challenge balanced inside and out, you will then experience true loving connections with others, and share your unique gifts, skills and abilities for the betterment of humanity.

Inspirational Connections

Inspirational connections are internally driven. They come from being consciously aligned with what is most meaningful and significant in your life. Nothing drives your inspiration more than knowing and acting on your highest core values and the purpose you were born to express. In order to live an inspired life with a sense of confidence, it is important to answer these questions;

- Who am I, and what do I want to do with my life?
- What do I love to do?

Get very quiet when you ask yourself these questions and listen carefully. Write down your answers in your inspirational journal. This is how you find your inspiration that comes from within.

Loving Connections

Loving connections always starts with you. It is a choice to have a loving connection. Having a loving connection with yourself has the most meaningful and healing influences on your mind-body system. Every cell vibrates in harmony. True health is the natural result of this harmonic vibration. When there is a lack of love, there is discord, harshness, and unhappiness that follows and may result in disease. Loving connections with yourself comes from allowing yourself to feel love, being loved, and saying loving things to yourself. In this moment, be okay with where you are right now and practice loving yourself. Being kind to yourself with a loving connection, and showing yourself appreciation, is the gateway for attracting the results you desire.

Strategies for Dealing with Difficult Relationships.

Difficult people usually lack a kind and loving relationship with themselves. They may not feel valued or loved and experience too much challenge and not enough support. They may not be living according to their own values or purpose and have become reactionary.

If you have relationship difficulties in your life, take a look at how you are reacting to them. Notice what you're saying to yourself about them. Notice how you are feeling about what you are saying.

Write down what you're saying and feeling. Then notice the benefits to being in a relationship with that person. Be clear and honest about what you are getting out of the relationship.

Use the breakthrough tapping process in chapter 7 to help you let go of any negative emotional reactions, feelings, or sensations that you are experiencing. This will help to release and dissolve your highly charged emotional states and one-sided perceptions. Once you have dissolved these negative feelings and reactions, then find some good things to say about them. See their good qualities and attributes.

"People treat you exactly the way you unconsciously treat yourself. Their outer mannerism towards you reflects your inner mannerism, so one of the most powerful ways to transform your life is to become consciously aware of your beliefs and feelings about yourself." - John Demartini

Affirmations for Deeper Loving Connections

I attract loving people in my life because
I love myself deeply.
I lovingly nurture and care for myself.
Equal amounts of support and challenge
help me to grow and be my best.
The more I express my divine purpose, the
more I am inspired.
I allow a loving connection to flow within
me and around me.

Inner Knowing

"Knowing yourself is the beginning of all wisdom." - Aristotle

Inner knowing comes from a still mind observing your thoughts and feelings in your body. When you observe your thoughts, ask yourself;

- How true is that thought?
- Does it align with what you value?
- Does it support a self-loving connection?
- Does it express kindness and appreciation for yourself?
- Does that thought/belief position you in a place of integrity or out of integrity?

Then check in with your feelings and ask; How does that feel? Scan your body to see if there is a reaction or sensation. This is because your thoughts create feelings, and your feelings create messages in your body. It is a cause and effect chain reaction. When you become aware, you know what is right for you at any given moment. This is real control. When you are not aware, you operate from old conditioned behaviors and reactions. This is not being in control.

Trust Yourself and your Abilities

Stop second-guessing yourself. Other people's options may only be serving them and may not be in your best interest. You can discover all the answers you seek from within. Continue to connect with yourself at a deep loving level. If you feel empowered, go for it. If you feel yucky, then explore other possibilities. How you feel matters. Trust is expecting the best to happen and believing in your ability to create what you want. Know you deserve to have it. You can develop trust by putting your ideas into action, getting feedback, seeing the results, and making new choices.

Awareness

Awareness is being conscious and focused on something specific in the present moment. Being aware of your thoughts, the words you speak, and the actions you demonstrate can support the congruent flow of your life's mission. When there is no awareness, there is an absence of connection and presence that limits the self from making new and different choices. Without awareness, the mind will wander without direction, defaulting to old subconscious programming and conditioning from the past. Awareness is one of the keys to making changes to the things that do not serve your higher purpose. Awareness will give you a choice to focus on the things that will make the biggest difference and allow you to break free from the old subconscious programs that you no longer require.

Seeing Both Sides

Seeing both sides of a situation or scenario is aligning with the universal laws of equilibrium. The law of balance states that there is a divine balance in everything. It's as simple as day and night, sun and moon, male and female; there are two sides. Seeing only one side of any situation creates an imbalance in the mind-body system. It's delusional and unrealistic to expect that there is only one side, one way to be, or one way to do things. This is how a fixed mindset is created. When you begin to see both sides, you see the perfection of your life. Everything happens for a reason.

Reset Yourself

Tune in to the smartest part of you. Tuning into yourself during quiet, reflective times like meditation and other mindful practices is very beneficial. Giving yourself permission every day to have these quiet moments can soothe away any irritations, transform how you feel into peace, and give you a sense of freedom.

You can reset when you find the time for stillness and quietude and allow the inspiration to flow through you. You will feel rested, rejuvenated, and your thoughts will be fresh and clear. When you have had time away from a challenging project, you will see it with a fresh new perspective.

"An awareness of one's mortality can lead you to wake up and live an authentic, meaningful life." - Bernie Siegel

Affirmations for Being Aware

My mind and body are listening to every thought.
I listen to my thoughts, and I'm watchful of my body.
I trust my intuitive self that is operating
for the greater good.
The more I am aware, the more I can take
the right action for me.
When I see both sides of any situation, I
remain balanced.
Making time to reset restores and
rejuvenates my whole being.

Powerful Self-Love Habits

"You, yourself, as much as anybody in the entire universe, deserve your love and affection." - Buddha

Being in a state of self-awareness and self-love is the foundation for greater personal and professional success. Practice this state often. Practice is the only way that self-love becomes conditioned as part of your essence. When you condition self-love, it becomes your natural, normal state of being. Practice makes permanent. So, the question is, what state are you going to practice?

Read through the list below and implement one that will make the biggest difference to your life today.

1. Practice being in a self-loving state at will. Practicing self-love habits requires you to prioritize it in your life. Loving yourself is a skill that can be mastered. You become aware automatically of self-respect, compassion, and heart-centered openness. Awareness of these qualities will enhance your health, wellbeing, relationships, and you will have a deeper connection with what matters most. Practice in a mirror and say, "I love you. You look wonderful today." or pick some affirmations that resonate with you.

2. Take time out for your precious self to quieten your mind. Peace and quietude are imperative for clarity, insightfulness, and mindfulness. Quietening the mind requires setting some time aside, especially when you are busy. Make and take the time; it is important. Here is a guided meditation I created that will help you get centered and calm in just a few minutes.

Here is the link. Calm and Peace Meditation
https://www.youtube.com/watch?v=J5a0-Tw9tUI/

3. Become aware of what you value the most. Your values are important, as they determine your life direction and purpose. Doing something that resonates with you, that makes you feel alive, excited, or inspired is one of the most important self-loving things you can do. Knowing what your values are is the first step in giving your life meaning and purpose.

Self-Love Habits Exercise

To get you started, answer the following questions:

- What inspires you? What are your top values, and what are you trying to fulfill with them?
- Why do you value what you value?
- Then, after each answer; Why is that important?

Inspiration and clarity occur when your direction, attention, and focus are aligned with your unique purpose. To learn more about how to realize your values and purpose, head to:

https://www.totalintegratedtherapy.com/activate-your-unique-purpose-course/

"There is no scarcity of opportunity to make a living at what you love; there's only scarcity of resolve to make it happen." - Dr Wayne Dyer

Affirmations for Self-Love

I love myself and my unique qualities.
I am beautiful, inside, and out.
I trust and follow my heart.
I choose to love, honor and accept myself.
I live, love, learn and grow.
I prioritize my self-love habits.
Self-love is living by what is meaningful
and inspiring to me.

Chapter 2
Align your Mind-Body

You
Your True Self Exercise
Be Aware of Resistance
Implementation Exercise
Affirmations

Mind-Body Intelligence
The Body Reactions
Listening
Be the Observer
Essential Movement
Affirmations

Choices and Decisions
Discover Your Favorites Exercise
Affirmations

Chapter 2
Align your Mind-Body

"Let yourself be silently drawn by the strange pull of what you really love. It will not lead you astray." - Jalaluddin Mevlana Rumi

You

How you see yourself will create the level of success that you achieve in your life. It's important to discover who you truly are, which is far beyond who you think you are or what you may have experienced in your life up to this point.

Your physical body is an expression and extension of who you are, but you are not your body. You think, but you are not your thoughts. You feel, but you are not your feelings. You are the observer.

It has been said that you are a spiritual being having a human experience. The problem is that your view of the world and yourself has been created and reduced to a limited version of yourself over your lifetime. The result is that you become distorted by conditioning and distracted by key events throughout your life. These events have created the lens that you view your life and life experiences. This is how you have learned to process the world. This is called perception. Your personal version of reality.

You are the most important person in your own life, despite what you have been led to believe. It is only you that can make your dreams come true. You control your own success by not taking a back seat in your life. When you choose your true self first, you jump back into the driver's seat of your own life. Putting yourself first means listening to what matters to you. Being the light in your own life means shining that light on what is most important and valuable to you. This will guide you to fulfillment, so you will naturally want to be of service to the world.

Your True Self Exercise

To discover more about yourself and who you truly are, answer these questions in your inspirational journal:

- *Who are you really?*
- *How would you describe yourself to someone else?*
- *What are your unique gifts, skills, and abilities?*

When you know the answers to these questions, you begin to unfold the mystery and wonderment of you. Life is a work in progress, and you are perfectly perfect in all your imperfections. If you don't know who you are, it is easy to get lost like an empty vessel wandering around trying to find your way. Who you really are is not what you have accomplished in the way of awards or degrees you have attained. Knowing your true self is about the real you and what makes you unique.

It is time to get clear about what you want. Most people are so focused on what they don't want that they never take the time to find out what they do want. Loving what you do and doing what you love will give you the energy, inspiration, and purpose to drive your success in every area of your life. When there is an imbalance in any one of these areas, it can create stress and tension. You have to know what you want to create before you can bring it about. If you don't know what you want, you will be like a ship without a rudder, and the universe and other people will fill your time, and you may not like the results. So many people in the world today are doing work that they dislike, and as a result, are miserable and dissatisfied with life. That's because they never took the time to find the answers to these questions.

- *What do you want? (In terms of personal growth, health, career, relationships, spirituality, finances, social interaction, home environment, hobbies, and fun)?*
- *What do you love?*
- *What makes your heart sing?*
- *What inspires you?*
- *What motivates you?*
- *What makes you laugh?*

When you know what it is you want to create, you can start attaining it. Many roads lead to the same destination, so knowing "how" at this point does not matter. What matters is finding the right fit for you. That is why these questions will help to guide and open your mind to new possibilities.

Now, let's go a little deeper. Answer these questions for every answer above:

- *Why do you want that? (answer this question for everything you want from the question above.)*

- *Why is that important to you?* (follow up with this question to dig deeper.)

When you know without a doubt why you want to do, be, or have that thing, your excitement will be flowing. Your big why will inspire you to take massive action. Taking action is how you move forward in the direction of fulfillment. Not knowing why you are doing something or why you want to do it is like playing the lottery. The chances of winning are astronomically low, and the odds are stacked heavily against you in creating what you want. Sometimes, we get lucky, but most of the time we distract ourselves from what we truly want to accomplish and end up going down the wrong road.

When I started to focus on what mattered to me most, my life truly unfolded in amazing ways. It continues to unfold beyond my wildest dreams. Some of my experiences have been extraordinary, and some have been ordinary. Being in the right place at the right time and meeting people who have helped me to grow, develop, and uncover who I really am, has inspired me to do what I'm doing today. What I discovered was that what I do matters, and I am the creator of my life experiences.

Be Aware of Resistance

Listen to the internal feedback and the messages from your body. Be aware of any resistance to answering any of the questions above. Resistance shows up when there is some value or benefit to holding on to what you have inside. Just be aware of any resistance or triggers that may be trying to protect you by keeping you safe in the old familiar, habitual program. Resistance can halt the process of change and create a roadblock to the life you want to create. It's essential to let go of your resistance so you can set yourself free to be inspired and creative.

"When you are aware of your resistance, you can overcome any fears that may be holding you back from experiencing your higher mind." - Kim Ryder

When I let go of my old fears from the past, my life unfolded in incredible ways. Instead of my life feeling limited by what I thought I couldn't do, I began to see what was possible. With time my belief became one of anything is possible! In the past, even writing this book would have been impossible for me to conceive because of my limited thinking at that time. What I had to do is be uncomfortable for a while until I felt I could trust my inner-self in the process. My deep desire to help myself and help other people became so strong that I couldn't ignore it anymore, and I decided to take action.

Implementation Exercise

In the next exercise, write down your answers to these questions:

- What fears are holding you back from doing what you love or want?
- Notice the beliefs around those fears. Ask yourself, when did they start?
- How do you know it's true? How true is it now?
- Notice any discontent with not having what you want.

- *If you discover any limiting beliefs that persist, you can use the breakthrough tapping process in chapter 7 and dissolve the one-sided beliefs that have been holding you back.*
- *Now take a look at where you are and where do you want to be.*
- *Give yourself permission to change your mind and create a new stream of thinking. Believe you deserve to have what you want and desire.*

Answer the questions above and write them down in your inspirational journal, so you can review, get clear, and refine your answers. Congratulate yourself when you are finished for a job well done! You are learning more about the most important person in your life.

> *"You must be the change you wish to see in the world."* - Mahatma Gandhi

Affirmations to Align Myself

I am grateful for my life and present in this moment.
I am perfectly perfect in all my imperfections.
I love, honor, and respect my mind and body.
I love what I do, and I do what I love.
Accomplishing my dreams is easy when I know what they are and why.

Mind-Body Intelligence

"Whatever the mind thinks and believes the body experiences and expresses." - Dave Ryder

The mind-body connection is a complete system. The mind and body work together as one; whatever the mind thinks and believes, the body will experience and express. The body is our humble servant and has the great ability to heal or destroy itself. Within the human body, we have systems that run systems of systems. The whole body has an incredible intelligence organized and coordinated by the central nervous system, which is the master controller of all the essential dynamic functions in the amazing human body. Your mind and body is a complete system that functions according to how you think, what you believe, and your perception of the world.

The Body Reactions

The body reacts from perceptions of what you think about yourself, life, and relationships. We apply meaning to everything we experience in life, both internally and externally. This is how the body creates ease or dis-ease. All illnesses have an emotional component attached to them. This means there is an underlying emotional cause that has been repressed that is being expressed physically. Even though most of the time this emotional component is beyond awareness, whatever you think about, your body obeys and reacts. In other words, whatever you think about, you bring about in your body. Being self-aware is a skill developed through practice. We can cultivate this self-awareness and bring about optimal health and wellbeing.

Listening

Listen to what your body is communicating. When you listen carefully to the feelings, sensations, and emotional responses of what your body is saying, you will get feedback and body intelligence.

When you do not live by your highest values, it creates low-level vibrations and creates a negative energy drain on the mind-body system. This usually occurs because of self-imposed limitations from limited choices. The sympathetic nervous system is continually triggered by what you believe and perceive. Getting triggered comes from internal and external stimulus via thoughts, behaviors, and reactions to highly charged habitual emotional states.

If you continue to ignore your body's messages and warning signals and what you are doing to create them, your body will respond by creating illness, pain, and dis-ease. Our bodies were never built to sustain this kind of abuse, which is how people produce sickness and disease.

Be the Observer

Be an observer of yourself to become aware and understand what triggers you to feel the way you do. Releasing and forgiving past hurts, painful experiences and making peace with your past is very healing. When you no longer react, the body can do what it does best, which is to heal. When you hold on to these past hurts, you bring them into the present. As a result, you cannot unfold the future, and your body will degenerate.

Observe with an awareness of what you are doing to yourself inside yourself via your thoughts, words, and actions. You are always producing results successfully, whether you like the results or not. It's imperative to be mindful and aware of what you are doing to yourself inside yourself. Then you can take back control of your life and produce results that will benefit you.

I have witnessed two friends that were diagnosed with terminal cancer and given a year to live. One friend decided to do the inner work and reset into a loving path, aligned with her truth. She is still here today, seven years later, and thriving in her life. The other friend went down the route of medical intervention but rejected the inner work. She died at the young age of 42, within two years of the diagnosis.

The human body has the incredible ability to heal, rejuvenate, and restore itself when you hit the reset button of self-love in the present moment. Medical science is slowly coming around to the idea that feelings and emotions play a critical role in the healing process.

Essential Movement

Movement is necessary for our physiology, psychology, and neurology. The whole mind-body system benefits from movement. Movement has been a big part of my life. As a child, my brother and I loved to ride our three-wheeler bikes together. We had so many fabulous adventures together, and sometimes we would be gone all day long. In my teens, I played a lot of basketball. In my early twenties, I began to sing and dance and play music in bands. At 28 years old, I started going to a regular integral Hatha Yoga class, and my body and mind loved it. The experience was like coming home to myself. Everything clicked, and I felt so blessed with the teachers that were there to teach me. It was the first time in my life that I felt peace and truly connected to my mind, body, and the divine source. I gained clarity, focus, and my true path. The best thing of all is that I didn't know that I was going to receive those gifts. When I started connecting to my true self, I got the profound changes and shifts in my life that I was always searching for outside of myself. Yoga is not about the body beautiful it is about connecting to who you truly are. Try Yoga for yourself!

It is also vital to be mindful about how to rejuvenate your body with nourishing food and life-giving water. Both are essential for healthy living. Good nutritious food is the fuel of your life force. Water is the essence of the human body, so we need to replenish it consciously and consistently. The body cannot function properly or effectively with only the occasional glass of water here and there. Otherwise, the body will start to fail and malfunction.

The air you breathe, the water you drink, the food you eat, your daily routine, and the habits you adopt contribute to your mind-body health and wellness. Your overall health and fitness are a long-term commitment, and the key is consistency. Furthermore, it's important to take stock and assess whether you are taking steps in the direction of attaining and maintaining a healthy lifestyle. Everything you do will take you on a path to health and wellness or dis-ease and discomfort. You get to choose!

Affirmations to Align Mind and Body

I listen to my mind and body and reset into love.
My mind and body work as a complete system.
Moving my body creates balance and freedom.
I give my body the fuel it needs to thrive.
Miracles are expressions of love.

Choices and Decisions

"There are two primary choices in life: to accept conditions as they exist, or accept the responsibility for changing them." - Denis Waitley

Choices give you the options to make decisions. Decisions are the results of processing choices. Every decision-making process produces a final choice. Sometimes we may think we have made a bad choice in our relationship, career, situation, or where we live. But that's not the whole picture. Each one of our decisions gives us information and feedback and gives us results to learn from. For example, we never make a decision without it benefiting us in some way, whether we are aware of it or not. To make better decisions, we have to evaluate the results of previous decisions. All results are perfect either for our growth or our enjoyment. Past experiences can create a one-sided perception skewing our view of our current choices and creating limited options. One-sided perceptions come from being emotionally conditioned to past programming and outdated states of mind.

For example, I worked with a client that was conditioned to believe, as a child, that it was her responsibility to make the men in her life happy. The man she attracted to be her husband believed that it was her job to make him happy. The result was that she could never do enough to make him happy. They were both miserable, and the relationship didn't last. What needed to happen in order for her to produce different results was to change those early conditioned programs. Then she could make new choices based on different information. Now she chooses to be in a loving and supporting relationship with herself, which allowed her to attract a more supporting and loving man that didn't rely on her for his happiness. Happiness is a choice. It is an internal state of being that cannot be produced by someone else.

Making high-quality choices that resonate with your highest core values is very powerful. You will feel a difference vibrationally in your mind and body. When you make high-quality choices and decisions, you create a vibrational state that empowers you to go in the direction of fulfillment.

I had made some major decisions in my life that had transitioned me to live in multiple countries around the world. Each time I moved, there was a great adjustment period where I doubted my choices and decisions, but each experience was a tremendous personal growth period in my life. My decisions guided me to have new experiences to develop new skills and expand my horizons.

Discover Your Favorites Exercise

Answer the questions below to discover what you prefer. Your answers will give you some great insight and open the doors for new possibilities. The more you write and express these questions, the more clarity you will have.

- *What is your favorite thing to do?*
- *What do you love to do that gives you the greatest joy?*
- *What would you like to do that you are not doing yet?*
- *What is one thing you like about being you?*

Now pick the one thing that will make the biggest difference in your life.
Then continue by asking;

- *How will that benefit me?*
- *And why is that important?*

Write the answers in your inspirational journal and continue until you have finished your list. Reflect on your answers.

"You and I are essentially infinite choice-makers. In every moment of our existence, we are in that field of all possibilities where we have access to an infinity of choices." - Deepak Chopra

Affirmations Align with My Choices and Decisions

I choose the activities that connect
me to joyful states.
It is safe for me to decide on the choices
that serve my higher purpose.
Every choice I make is benefiting me in some way.
I make choices that resonate with my
highest core values.
The things I create are even better than
I imagined them to be.
I choose to live an inspirational life.

Chapter 3
Align with Focus and Clarity

Focus
The Path
Your Thoughts
Your Words
Your Feelings
Taking Action
Meaningful Action Exercise
Affirmations

Clarity
Mindfulness
Mindful Practice
Meditation
Being Awake
Being Deliberate
Affirmations

Chapter 3
Align with Focus and Clarity

"The ability to remain calm and focused in stressful situations is central to making positive decisions" - Goldie Hawn

Focus

Focus is being one-pointed. Let go of the distractions and the things that are not important. We can easily get drawn into other people's dramas, problems, and other distractions. Frustration can occur when you don't focus on what is most important and meaningful. Focus is putting your attention on your chosen goal and taking action to generate the results you want to create. This focus applies to goals in all areas of your life. Consistently reaffirm what is important to you by purposefully directing your focus back to your value-based goals. This will encourage you to take action in the direction of fulfillment.

The Path

The path you choose is yours. Embracing your unique values will guide your decisions and steer your life down the right path. You can have faith and courage in your values. Keep reminding yourself of the big reasons "Why" you are traveling down your chosen path. It's important to take each new step one at a time and remember there are no mistakes, just results and learning experiences. You can always make improvements as you go. There were times in my life when I didn't know why I was traveling down a particular path, and sometimes I didn't like the destination or results. I started writing down a list of pro's and con's and asking myself the "Why" questions - *Why do I want that? Why is that important to me?* These questions helped me make better decisions. When you don't know where you're going, where you end up is out of your control. Setting a directional path is like having an internal GPS for your life. A directional path based on your highest values will take you from where you are now to where you want to go.

Your Thoughts

Thoughts are powerful. The power of the mind is one of the greatest strengths you possess, and this power starts with the quality of your thoughts.

The thoughts that pass through your mind are responsible for your feelings, perceptions, and experiences. Your thoughts determine your focus and awareness. They influence what you learn, your plans, ideas, goals, desires, and everything else that happens in your life. Predominant thoughts create a response in the body that affects your moods, experiences, behaviors, actions, and reactions, even though most of the time, you are completely unaware that this occurs. Focus your mind by directing your thoughts to one positive action at a time. By maintaining your focus on one action, you will make steady progress toward your goals. When you focus your mind's power on what is most meaningful, your thoughts become empowered.

Your Words

Your words are your affirmations; they can be healing or harmful. Your thoughts need to match your words so that you take inspired action that brings you to what you want to create. We all speak countless words every day, often paying very little attention to the words themselves. It's important to realize that you are creating your world by the words that you speak. Practice speaking empowering words. Then feel them and make them true for you. If they don't resonate, then let them go and find ones that do.

Your Feelings

Your feelings are your best indicator of whether you are in or out of alignment. It's important to listen when you have that niggling feeling that something is off. Many people go through life as slaves to their own feelings and emotions. They don't realize that feelings and emotions are the results of their thoughts. This is because people get conditioned to let their emotions be in control instead of being in control of emotions. So, if you want to feel differently, decide how you want to feel, then create a new thought that will align with how you want to feel. Feelings can be interpreted as an internal barometer telling you if your thoughts align with your actions. If you feel uninspired, sad, bored, or frustrated, it's important to figure out what thoughts create that feeling. All of our feelings are clues to teach us something important about ourselves.

How you feel will influence what you do or don't do, and determine your outcome or results. How you feel will affect your behavior, attitude, and how you go about doing what you do. You can see why it's so important to get feelings under control. Feelings are the result and effect of what you think and tell yourself.

Taking Action

Taking action is one of the most important steps in making positive life changes. If you don't place a high value on a particular action, you'll tend to delay and postpone, or get frustrated and procrastinate altogether. Motivation signifies the reasons for people's actions, desires, and needs. If they need motivation to do something, then it comes from prioritizing a lower level value, and that can be exhausting. If you take action according to your highest core values, you will be inspired to jump out of bed with an abundance of energy and enthusiasm. If you are taking inspired action you, will know when something is right for you. By taking action, you will overcome your fears and expand beyond your comfort zone. action taking makes taking meaningful action exponentially easier in all areas of your life.

Meaningful Action Exercise

Take meaningful action daily. Write down the action that will help to bring you closer to your goal in your inspirational journal:

- *What one action will make the biggest difference today?*
- *If I do this today, what will happen in the long term?*

"The key to success is to focus our conscious mind on things we desire not things we fear." - Brian Tracy

Affirmations to Align Thoughts, Feelings, and Actions

I direct my thoughts on one empowering
action at a time.
Step by step, I make the necessary changes that
change my world.
I am not defined by what I feel.
Words create my world, and I choose to create a
world I want to live in.
I speak the words that resonate
with my highest values.

Clarity

"Doubt everything. Find your own light." - Gautama Buddha

Clarity means clearness. It's a state of being clear and easy to understand. Having clarity about what you think and what you want to accomplish is an essential step in taking responsibility for your current pursuits. Clarity gives you the freedom to create better possibilities for future goals that will take you to where you want to go. Mental clarity occurs in the present moment when we are free from disturbance and distractions. Clarity is essential when you are looking for direction in your life.

In our world today, we are being bombarded with information overload from multiple sources, filling the space in our minds with a lot of unimportant trivia. When our minds are full, it is hard to think clearly. Having clarity will reduce frustration, misunderstanding, and unwanted results.

Mindfulness

Mindfulness is paying attention to what matters now, so that you can create a balance between your thoughts, feelings, emotions, words, and actions. The mind is the creator of all actions and all functions in the body. Stress is the body's reaction to perception. Being mindful of your stress reactions and triggers can help to control and release them. One of the simplest ways to direct the mind is by focusing on breathing. When I need to do something important, I take three deep breaths, I feel my feet on the ground and relax my body. Before you go and do an important task, like an exam, meeting a new boss, speaking in front of a group, stop and take three deep, slow breaths. Breathe deeply into your diaphragm and then slowly exhale. Deep slow breaths will help you be connected, confident, and present in the moment so that you are ready, calm, and centered. Mindfulness creates equanimity, a state of mental calmness, composure, and consistency, especially in challenging situations.

Mindful Practice Exercise

Practicing the quality of being clear, calm, and absent of thought for at least fifteen minutes a day will help bring about a peaceful and clear state of mind.

It is important to find a quiet, comfortable space where you will not be disturbed. Sit in a comfortable position and close your eyes. Then focus your attention on the flow of breath, in and out of your nose, 25 times. Focusing on breathing will bring you into awareness of the present moment and help you to feel centered. Practicing this calm state of being will direct your mind towards equanimity, clarity, and peace. Give yourself the gift of quiet solitude in a serene space, and you will find clarity, direction, and peace of mind.

Meditation

Meditation means contemplation and reflection. Meditation is a practice in which an individual focuses their mind or induces a mode of consciousness to realize some benefit or as an end in itself. Meditation is a beautiful way to gain control of your state of mind. It is where the person meditating is in a state of bliss and one-pointed focus. The more conscious you are, the more control you have over your thoughts. This is what it means to know your true self. Becoming aware of your impulses, urges, and habits allow you to gain control over them. As you become more conscious of your own unconscious states and increase your awareness of what's going on in your mind and body, you become empowered and will enjoy having the ultimate control over your life. What you discover through the practice of meditation is that you are not the contents of your mind's activity; you are much more.

Being Awake

Being awake to the world around you is an active conscious process. Regular meditation and contemplation in silence is the practice of being awake. How many times have you driven somewhere and not remembered how you got there? How many times a day do you go off into a daydream? Being awake gives you more control of your life so you can direct your dreams and make them a reality. When you are awake, you are consciously connected to the present moment.

Being Deliberate

Being deliberate is taking action consciously and intentionally. When you do things in a deliberate way, it means that you have thoughtfully planned your actions in a purposeful way. Deliberate action is a means to an end that will produce intentional results. Right now, at this moment, I am deliberately writing this book to share information, knowledge, and wisdom that will help you to be more loving and connected to your true self.

Creating conscious clarity with conviction is the act of following through with taking inspired and deliberate action. Tune in to the direction that you want to go. It's good to check in with yourself to see if what you are doing feels good. Then continue moving forward and ask yourself: What can I do today that will help me to move forward? And by moving forward, how will that benefit my life?

"With mindfulness, you can establish yourself in the present in order to touch the wonders of life that are available in that moment." - Thich Nhat Hanh

Affirmations to Align with Mindfulness

Clarity comes when I focus being in
the present moment.
I pay attention to what matters now
and produce better results.
As I increase my awareness, I feel empowered.
When I am in the present moment, I
am consciously connected.
When I am being deliberate, I am being intentional.

Chapter 4
Inspired Action

Meaningful Purpose
Core Values
Uncover Your Values
Reveal Your Core Values Exercise
The Universal Law of Attraction
Principle Powers
The Benefits
Affirmations

Power Rituals
My Morning Power Ritual
Create Your Power Ritual Exercise
Habit and Routines
Schedule Time
Confidence and Certainty
50 Benefits Exercise
Affirmations

Chapter 4
Inspired Action

"What other people label or might try to call failure, I have learned is just God's way of pointing you in a new direction" - Oprah Winfrey

Meaningful Purpose

When you have a meaningful purpose, that purpose is what you think about, dream about, and is the essence of your core values. When you define your purpose and act upon it, only then can you become the best version of yourself and achieve your true potential.

"There is no scarcity of opportunity to make a living at what you love; there's only scarcity of resolve to make it happen" - Wayne Dyer

Those who do not have a clear purpose tend to go around in circles feeling stuck and frustrated. This is true for a lot of people as they cycle through life without knowing what their purpose is or why they are doing what they're doing. Without a clear purpose, there is aimless wondering without meaningful focus. There is also a tendency to follow a path of less resistance, which keeps people stuck in a familiar comfort zone. A purpose is a focused mission and is driven by the inspiration of your highest core values. Purpose is what gives you the propulsion to go where you need to go.

Core Values

Core values reflect what is truly important. Your values are the guiding principles that dictate behavior and action in a meaningful direction. They can help you determine if you are on the right path or not. Your core values are the cornerstone of your foundation, and when you operate within your core values, life flows in the direction of fulfillment.

Uncover Your Values

Your values are significantly important and grossly undervalued. Every time you set a goal that is not in alignment with your values you decrease the probability of success. Most people get stuck doing jobs they don't enjoy because it never occurred to them that they could choose work that is in alignment with what is most important to them. As a result, they get by in a status quo position and lifestyle, denying their wishes, hopes, and desires for something better. Others get stuck because of obligations to others or blindly assuming financial success and material things that will bring them what they think they want.

What you value the most is one of the things that makes you unique. Your values are the driving force behind living a purposeful life. When we deny or suppress our values, we get stuck living someone else's. This results from not living in alignment with what is most meaningful and precious. This also results in being dissatisfied and unfulfilled in life. When you identify your values, you can steer your life toward a fulfilling life driven by purpose. Your values don't come from your family, boss, society, or anything else outside of you. Living by your values is the most direct and beneficial way of meeting your own needs and igniting inspiration. It can cut out years of needless therapy. This is because you are tapping into the secret sauce of what inspires you and lights you up inside. By staying true to your values, you are honoring yourself in the highest order.

Reveal Your Core Values Exercise

Your core values relate to what you value the most at the deepest level. Please select 3-5, and put in order what is most important to you. Here are some ideas.

Achievement	Gratitude	Potential
Adventure	Giving In-service	Play
Beauty	Health	Productivity
Being the best	Honesty	Primary Relationship
Challenge	Independence	Reliability
Comfort	Inner peace	Respect
Courage	Intelligence	Research
Creativity	Integrity	Study
Curiosity	Intimacy	Sustainable
Education	Independently Wealthy	Spirituality
Expression	Inspiration	Success
Empowerment	Joy	Time freedom

Environment	Love	Teaching
Family	Learning	Travel
Financial freedom	Leadership	Variety
Fitness	Performance	Wellbeing
Friendship	Personal growth	Work Ethic

Now, complete the following to help you refine your values in your inspirational journal.

1. *In your personal work and home space, write down three of the most meaningful items in that space.*
2. *Write down the top three things you spend the majority of your time on.*
3. *Write down the top three things you spend the most energy on that energize you.*
4. *Write down the top three things you spend the majority of your money on.*
5. *Now, look at your list and write down what each one of your answers means to you.*
6. *Now, find the deeper meaning of each of your answers. Give three reasons and describe why each item on your list is a core value.*
7. *What is it that you gain from each one of those things?*
8. *Make sure it resonates true to you and feels congruent.*

This process will make you aware of what you want to consciously align your life with. This is the key to identifying the significant qualities that are uniquely yours. You empower your life when you are connected and operate from your highest values. Your highest values are the driving force behind your purpose and mission in life. When you are in alignment with your magnificent unique values, life energy flows towards personal abundance and perpetual richness.

The Universal Laws of Attraction

The Universal Laws of Attraction are guiding us day in and day out, whether we are aware of it or not. You've heard the saying, "Whatever you think about, you bring about". Your thoughts are important and you have to be mindful about what you are putting out in the world as you may be unwittingly creating what you don't want. Attracting what you want in your life has a few fundamental principles that will make all a difference when applied.

- *Firstly, it is important to know what you want to create. The more detailed the better.*
- *Secondly, knowing why you want what you want and how that is going to benefit you. Again, you need to be detailed.*
- *Thirdly, imagine how it feels for you to have that already*
- *and how your life will change as a result.*
- *Lastly, it's important not to be attached to any outcome or rely on a result for how you feel.*

It is time to get clear about what and why. Knowing what you want and why will give you deeper insights into your intentions and motives for fueling what it is that you want to create. This is crucial because when you leave out specific details that limit clarity, you open yourself to situations that allow others to fill in the blanks. Furthermore, it's key to believe you can have and deserve to live a fulfilling life. It is also essential to be aware of any resistance to creating what you want and clear that out. Otherwise, you may never feel fulfilled. When you clear out resistance, you are open to receive and allow abundance to flow with ease and grace.

Principle Powers

Principle Powers relate to your *Values, Purpose, Vision*, and *Mission* in life. Your Principle Powers are the driving force behind who you are at your deepest core self. When you activate and connect to all of your Principle Powers, you live a consciously empowered life that unfolds in miraculous ways. You embrace creativity, flow from inspired states, enjoy boundless energy and spiritual guidance that all come from within you. Your Principle Powers are uniquely yours, and everyone has them. It is a matter of uncovering what is already there, just waiting to unfold. Many people think that enlightenment is the pinnacle of life. Real enlightenment starts when you realize and live by your unique Principle Powers. This means having a clear vision of what you want to create, having a mission that inspires you to wake up and want to share it with the world.

The Benefits

The benefits of aligning with your Principle Powers is to empower you to connect to your deepest core self. When there is alignment in all areas of your life, there is a congruent flow of positive energy in a purposeful direction.

You can manifest what you want to create when you can declare it without a shadow of a doubt. When manifesting, it is vital to express what you want to create, believe that it is possible, and intend to have it. It is also important to be in a relaxed state of being. Remember to be as detailed as you can about what you want to create and imagine that you already have it. Then begin to notice how it would feel to create it in your life.

Once again, create the space for magnetizing what you want to create in your life. Then, visualize having created it, and notice how it will change your life. Always check for and remove any resistance in having those changes in your life. Letting go of any attachments to the outcome or results allows you to receive what is happening without resistance. What you are doing is allowing the results to unfold without getting emotionally attached.

"Dedicate your life to a cause that inspires you and also greatly serves others. Master plan your life. If you don't fill your day with high priorities, it will automatically become filled with low priorities." - John Demartini

Affirmations for Inspired Action

I set my intention and get clear on
my goals and aspirations.
Attracting what I want to create is easy
when I know the what and why.
When I connect to my Principle Powers, my life
unfolds in miraculous ways.
I deserve to have the very best in my life.
Inspiration flows easily and effortlessly when I align
with my purpose.

Power Rituals

"Many successful people get up before 6am in the morning. They have rituals. They exercise, stretch, organize their day, and walk through that series of rituals." - Brian Tracy

A ritual is a sequence of consistent activities involving gestures, words, or objects done in a sacred place and performed according to a set sequence. Historically rituals have been an important part of our society in a variety of ways. Many people go to a place of worship, or some have a specific daily ritual or practice meaningful to them.

A *Power Ritual* is where you practice a consistent sequence of intentional and meaningful activities that automatically draws you to achieving your goal. A Power Ritual brings inspiration, energy, and a healthy state of mind and body so you can produce the results you want.

For me, I created a morning *Power Ritual* of meditation, jogging, and Yoga. This helps me keep my body in shape, it brings calmness to my mind and sets me up for the day ahead.

My Morning Power Ritual

I personally like having a morning ritual, it sets my day up for success.
1. On awakening while still in bed, I think about the things I'm grateful for, my beautiful family, my wonderful life, the work I love to do, and the abundance that my life expresses.
2. I have some warm water and a hot cup of tea.

3. I love to meditate to connect deeply with my heart and soul. I meditate on the stillness of the space between the cosmic flow of the universe. It's where my inspiration flows, and insights to challenges unfold. I usually need a notebook by me, so that I can jot down any insightful inspiration.
4. I get warmed up for the day with movements of Yoga, and jogging. These positive activities are an important part of my ritual as they reset and stimulate all the systems in my body and recalibrate my mind.
5. I practice a few positive affirmations for focusing my thoughts and condition my mind for a successful day.
6. Reading an inspirational book or quotations reminds and inspires me to take action.

My morning Power Ritual is around one hour to an hour and thirty minutes. Then I sit outside if the weather is good to have my breakfast, welcome the new day, and enjoy my garden. Develop a morning ritual that is congruent with you and is aligned with what you enjoy is important. Open your mind and give yourself this gift. You'll be so glad you did!

Create Your Power Ritual Exercise

Right now, in your inspirational journal, create your own personal morning power ritual. Create a list of meaningful activities you enjoy and need. These activities will give you the energy and clarity that will take you in the right direction. Develop consistency in doing your power ritual every day.

Habit and Routine

As humans, we are all creatures of habit and routine. It's natural to have a set of "habitual routines" because if we don't, our lives will become chaotic. Some habits can be good, like brushing your teeth twice a day, or exercising, while other habits are unpleasant or unhealthy, like smoking or biting your fingernails. Your habits, good or bad, can affect your physical, mental, and emotional states.

For example; If you are in the habit of getting up late, rushing to work, eating on the run, or drinking coffee to keep going all day, this can create a lot of stress. Likewise, if you are in the habit of using drugs or alcohol to cope with stress, your body will eventually break down and get sick. In contrast, if you have a regular schedule of eating, going to bed, and exercising, this creates good healthy habits.

The good news is bad habits can be broken any time and exchanged for good healthy habits. Developing good habits start when you decide to do things differently and consistently, enabling you to express how you want to be and feel. Your good habits will take you to your goals automatically.

Schedule Time

Schedule time to prioritize the most meaningful and important tasks first. In our modern world life can seem very busy, happening at a fast rate. Take time to plan the things you want to have happen and put them on your calendar every week. It is important to block out time for priority activities, so you can say, "no" to the things that are not important. Make time for your precious self and take the time to implement your Power Rituals. This will be life-changing on many levels.

Confidence and Certainty

Confidence is feeling appreciation and certainty about your own gifts, qualities, and abilities. It is being confident in your convictions. When you are certain, others will be certain too. They will hear it in your voice, your tonality. Others will see it in your eyes, and feel it. If you resonate with them, there will be no convincing required. They will just know it is right. Walk in your truth and live by your values, and others will be certain and confident too. This is an irresistible force that will allow you to communicate your intention with confidence and avoid misunderstanding.

50 Benefits Exercise

Now, write down 50 benefits of doing "the one thing" that will change your life. This will give you all the reasons why it's a good idea. Knowing why you want something will help you to get closer to accomplishing it. Knowing is not enough, you must take action and implement those changes. Knowing the why gives you the inspirational energy to take the action required. It is said that consistency over a period of time will help you to create this new empowering habit.

In a study by Philippa Lally, published in the European Journal of Social Psychology. It states; it can take anywhere from 18 to 254 days for a person to form a new habit and an average of 66 days for a new behavior to become automatic.

Challenge yourself consistently every day and create that new Power Ritual that will empower your life.

"I never could have done what I have done without the habits of punctuality, order, and diligence, without the determination to concentrate myself on one subject at a time." - Charles Dickens

Affirmations for Power Rituals

I give myself permission to take time out for me.
I let go of old unproductive habits and
create new empowering ones.
I prioritize what is meaningful to me,
so that I can reap the rewards.
I set myself up for success with Power Rituals.
I communicate my intention with
confidence and conviction.
My Power Rituals automatically
take me to my goals.

Step-by-Step

"When you dance, your purpose is not to get to a certain place on the floor. It's to enjoy each step along the way." - Wayne Dyer

Taking one step at a time will help you to get where you want to go in a steady and consistent way. There's an old Chinese proverb that says, "It is better to take many small steps in the right direction than to make a great leap forward only to stumble backward." By choosing a goal and breaking it up into steps, you increase the chance of achieving that end goal. Each step will take you progressively toward completing the goal.

Steps and milestones that take you from A to B

A |—|—|—|—|—|—| B

In order to write this book, I followed some basic steps that helped me go from "A" the conceptual idea to "B" the finished published book. I do this with every project, book, or course idea and it helps me to complete that project. Here is a simple template to move away from "A" by filling in the milestones that need to be completed so you can arrive at "B" your destination.

Moving Forward

When you are focused on a goal, moving forward takes you in the direction of that goal. It is important to remember that your actions need to be aligned with your highest priority and core value.

Otherwise, it becomes easy to wind up in procrastination land or lazyville. Focus onward and upward to where you are heading. The road to success is always under construction. You'll want to make sure you are on the right road and moving steadily forward.

Albert Einstein said, "Life is like riding a bicycle. To keep your balance, you must keep moving."

Rhythm and Flow

Getting into your rhythm is a state of flow or movement. Flow is characterized by the total absorption in what you are doing. It is when you are fully immersed in a feeling of energized focus and joy in the process of the activity that you're creating. After meditation, I get into flow states when the quietness in my mind clears the pathways for inspiration and flow.

Pace Yourself

Pace is important during times of concentrated work. Give yourself some time out. It doesn't matter what area of business or work you are doing, taking a break is a must. After every forty minutes of concentrated work take a mini break. Even if it is just 5 minutes to stop, stand up, stretch, sit in the sun, or meditate. Sometimes it is even helpful to take a short fifteen minute nap during the day. Checking in with your body and clearing your thoughts will help you rejuvenate your mind and body.

Ask yourself;
- *What is the next step that I can take?*

- *What is the one thing that will make the biggest difference right now?*

Narrow it down so you take one deliberate step at a time. Then the next, and the next, until you have arrived. Even if you arrive at the conclusion that you need to add an extra step to produce another result, write down your answers in your inspirational journal.

"The secret of getting ahead is getting started. The secret of getting started is breaking your complex, overwhelming tasks into small manageable tasks, and then starting on the first one." - Mark Twain

Affirmations for Moving forward

Each new step takes me where I want to go in a
steady and consistent way.
One small step in the right direction
empowers my life.
I bring about a flow state to energize
my mind and body with joy.
I pace myself and reconnect with my
mind and body regularly.

Chapter 5
Mindful Awareness

Conscious Awareness
Being Present
Your Gifts and Skills
Now is the Only Time
Your Existence
How You Matter Exercise
Affirmations
Allowing
Giving
Truth
Affirmations

Intention
Setting Clear Intentions
Clarity of Intention
Defining Your What, Why and How
Being Intentional
Your Intention Exercise
Intention Statement
Responsibilities
Personal Responsibility
Affirmations

Chapter 5
Mindful Awareness

"If your mind carries a heavy burden of past, you will experience more of the same. The past perpetuates itself through lack of presence. The quality of your consciousness at this moment is what shapes the future." - Eckhart Tolle

Conscious Awareness

Conscious awareness is a powerful tool for changing unconscious patterns. Consciousness is awareness of the thoughts in your mind. Awareness is when you become the observer of what you are doing inside your mind. Becoming aware of being aware brings about a higher state of consciousness. When you become aware of your limiting thoughts, beliefs, and behaviors you can then change your thought patterns in the present. Many people live their lives on auto pilot with no idea that their mental conditioning, what they think and believe, creates their experiences. They think life is happening to them, instead of being consciously aware that their thoughts and reactions to those thoughts are driving their experiences.

The only way I could change my patterns was to become aware of them and change them. I changed them by releasing those outdated belief systems that were disconnecting me from my true self and purpose.

This was not an overnight event but a steady and consistent learning and growth process. You can do the same thing when you become consciously aware of the ways you hold yourself back. Leverage your principle powers to produce meaningful change in an intentional way.

Being Present

Being present is a powerful habit to practice. To be present is to be here now. Your power is and will always be in the present moment. There is empowerment in the present moment and a deep awareness of yourself and your surroundings. The present moment is where your thoughts, focus, and attention can be directed to achieving what you want to create. In today's modern world, staying focused can be difficult as there are so many distractions. However, with practice and perseverance, we can achieve a state of presence amidst chaos. Being present with awareness is a skill that can give you clarity and focus to keep you on track with any project. Practicing being present will empower you to focus your mind and attention to make positive changes, and to avoid distractions so you can complete tasks and accomplish goals.

Your Gifts and Skills

Your gifts, skills, talents, and abilities that are uniquely yours. There may be people out in the world with similar attributes that do similar things, but there is a big difference, they are not you. Your gifts and skills are developed from your unique model of the world. How you see and represent the world as well as your personal experiences, determine what makes you unique. I remember comparing myself with other people, thinking they were somehow better than me. I discovered that even though other people may have done similar things, no one did it exactly the way I did it. So, let go of your comparisons because there is no comparison to you. When you compare yourself to others, it can make you feel inadequate and not good enough. Many people get caught up in the idea that they have to be just like everybody else. But in truth, you can't be everybody else. That is impossible! Comparing yourself with others only puts you down and is being unfair to yourself. By comparing yourself to the fantasy of others, you become discouraged and may never take the action necessary to reach your full potential.

Now is the Only Time

Now is the only time we are all given. Reliving the past or focusing on the imaginary future robs you of the now. When you focus on what you should have done better, you are experiencing the past that cannot be changed. To be more present, release your reactions to the past because the past is dead and over. In the present, you can change how you represent the past right now, by letting go of the emotional attachments to those experiences. This will free you to become inspired in the present and allow your future to unfold in miraculous ways. In the present, you can focus, plan, and be in creative flow states. There is nothing more joyful to me than being in a creative flow. Right now is where all the power is! You can embrace your true self now and step into a state of peace and joy.

Your Existence

Existence is the nature of being. You were born for a reason with a unique purpose. We are all born to be a continuation of the evolution of humanity.

How You Matter Exercise

Now, answer the following questions in your Inspirational Journal:

- *How do you matter in the world?*
- *Who do you matter to?*
- *How does what you do matter in the world?*

"Learn to enjoy every minute of your life. Be happy now. Don't wait for something outside of yourself to make you happy in the future. Think how really precious is the time you have to spend, whether it's at work or with your family. Every minute should be enjoyed and savored." - Earl Nightingale

Affirmations for Conscious Awareness

When I am consciously aware, I can transcend my
old unconscious patterns.
Being present helps me to stay on task.
In the present, I can focus, plan, and
be in creative flow states.
I was born with my unique purpose, for a purpose.
I embrace the power of the present moment.

Allowing

"Your own self-realization is the greatest service you can render the world." - Ramana Maharshi

Allowing is giving yourself permission to receive. All of us have a greatness within, and it is a gift to yourself and the world to express that greatness. You have a responsibility to allow the expression of what is inside you to percolate and manifest. You do not need anyone else's permission to be awesome. Give yourself permission and allow your magnificent self to shine and embrace the uniqueness that is you.

Giving

Giving is the act of transferring something without the expectation of receiving in return. You choose to give with loving intention without expectation. Giving is offering an open hand of generosity to someone in need or just because you can. The act of giving is a gift when there are no obligations or strings attached. Not all gifts are genuine as they may have invisible cables attached or a strong intention to get something in return. Give yourself the best gift of all, the gift of loving-kindness to be your magnificent self and express your heart's desires.

Truth

Truth is a belief that is accepted as true from your own personal version of reality. When you are true to yourself, you are being congruent with the essence of you. Being true to yourself is imperative for living with integrity. True self-expression is part of proclaiming your originality and authentic self. When you speak from your authentic self, integrity supports your wholeness by using truth to influence your life. In other words, your life demonstrates your essence aligned with integrity.

As a young child I learned it wasn't okay to express myself. I remember being forced to sit at the dinner table with my brother for hours into the night because we didn't like eating our mother's lumpy mashed potatoes. My mother would go to great lengths trying to make us eat. For example, she added green food coloring to the cold lumpy potatoes, which made it worse. The truth is, I like mashed potatoes, just not lumpy ones, let alone lumpy green ones. Back then, my dad was keen to train us in different sports, but he didn't express patience. There were many occasions while being trained, that I was scared to do what he wanted for fear of being hurt or rejected. I remember being scolded and crying so many times. Eventually I came to the conclusion that is was not safe to express myself because either way, I would get in trouble. In those early years, speaking up or expressing myself led to being screamed at, or worse. The disapproval expressed from my parents, and later by school teachers who used corporal punishment, created a belief in me that expressing myself would result in more pain and unpleasant experiences. This belief kept me feeling invisible much of my life and prevented me from expressing my true self. Fortunately, I was able to change that old belief and express myself the way I wanted to. Back then, the viewpoint was that children should be seen and not heard. That point of view cycled through many generations of my family. As a result, throughout my life, I felt a deep fear of rejection from others when expressing my needs. I spent much of my life putting others needs before my own which left me feeling empty, depleted, frustrated, and resentful.

As an adult, I felt a deep frustration from not living a purposeful life. I wanted to express myself, but what held me back was a dreadful fear that if I expressed myself the people closest to me would criticize or reject me. My fear of rejection and criticism held me back in so many areas of my life. Holding onto this fear also served the purpose of keeping me safe, as long as I played by those old rules. Sadly, being stuck in this old pattern of fear caused me to have continual stomach and digestive problems for most of my life.

To get back on the road of self-acceptance and speaking my truth, I had to honor myself and release the old fear pattern, that they will reject me if I don't follow their rules. I then aligned with my values and started to live a more meaningful life. Living in integrity allowed me to harmonize with my truth. Aligning myself began when I submerged myself in the practice of Integral Hatha Yoga in my late twenties. For the first time, I learned to go inside myself, be safe, and find peace within. Later I learned the art of releasing my subconscious programs through a process of tapping, which helped me to release the limitations that held me back for so long. Then I was able to attune myself and live in alignment with my meaningful values and purpose.

Whether you are being congruent or incongruent with yourself, you feel it inside. Your body is like the barometer of your congruence level. With awareness, you can become more conscious of the messages inside your own body. These body messages are expressed through sensations, feelings, and emotions. You can begin to notice when you are being incongruent by the feedback in your body. This is a wake-up call. You can feel it! Embedded in the walls of the stomach is an enteric nervous system that helps you sense environmental threats that influence your reactions and responses. This same influence can be felt in the body when there is a congruent or incongruent change in your internal environment. It's important to pay attention to the feedback your body is giving you, because your body is always listening and will respond perfectly.

"As we let our light shine, we unconsciously give other people permission to do the same. As we are liberated from our own fear, our presence actually liberates others."- Marianne Williamson

Affirmations for Self-Expression

I give myself permission to be magnificent, and I embrace my uniqueness.
I give myself the gift of loving-kindness.
I allow my magnificent self to shine.
I express my true self, and I shine.
I accept my own truth, and I listen for congruence in my body.

Intention

"Women, with their sure instincts, realized that my intention was to make them not just more beautiful but also happier." - Christian Dior

Intention is something that you aim to do or bring about. It's a state of mind that can be seen as directing one's mind and efforts consistently and attentively. Intention is actually a state of mind for the purpose in which you can act upon. Your energy flows where your focused attention and awareness goes. Your intention is the underlying purpose of where you are placing your awareness. Intention is the seed of creation planted in the mind that, when aligned with right action, allows your deepest intention to be fulfilled.

Setting Clear Intentions

Setting a clear intention is the first positive step of any successful creative venture. A conscious clear intention can greatly assist any creative effort, no matter how big or small. Setting an intention is very beneficial when creating new habits. Before I start any new habit, I set an intention that the new habit will be part of my lifestyle. For example, when I wanted to increase my water intake for improved heath, my intention was to feel rejuvenated and energized throughout the day. Now I have a water bottle that helps me track my intake and keeps me well hydrated all day long. I highly recommend you do the same.

Clarity of Intention

Clarity of intention combined with mindfulness and awareness is the most powerful mental creative force you have. One of my biggest aha moments was when I learned that I could set an intention that aligned my life with what I wanted to express. When I started setting purposeful intentions, it becomes one of the most powerful creative tools to change the course of my life.

Define Your What, Why, and How

Defining your what, why, and how will empower your intentions. Before starting any creative endeavor, it is essential that you take a look at your intention and what lies behind that intention. Clarity of intention not only means being able to state what you want to create verbally; it also means understanding why you want to create what you want. What you do is the tangible representation of your why. Your how, is the action steps you took to create what you did to make a difference. When you begin a new project knowing what and why is more important than how. A strong why drives you to take action and supports your determination to be consistent in your efforts, even through tough times. If you don't have a strong why, you may never start the project, and if you do start, the first major obstacle can stop you in your tracks. So, a powerful why strengthens your determination when you need it the most.

Being Intentional

Being intentional is knowing what you want to do, why you are doing it, and how it will change your life.

Being aware of what lies behind the intention of what you want, and how it will benefit you waters the seeds of that intention.

When you deliberately set an intention that is clearly expressed with aligned actions you activate the powerful flow of co-creation with the universe. It is also important to surrender your attachment to a particular result or outcome. Attachment signifies insecurity and fears. When you set an intention and let go of expectations, you announce your aspiration to the universe and release your creative power by igniting inspired action.

Clear Intention Exercise

Write down your aspirations and intentions in your Inspirational Journal. Be as specific as possible.
The more concentrated and specific your intention is, the more potent and abundant the result.

- *Write down what you want.*
- *Write down your intentions for what you want. (Use the intention statement below)*
- *Write down why that is important to you.*
- *Write down how it will feel when what you want becomes a reality.*

Intention Statement

Make an intention statement in the present tense.
My intention is....... Or I intend to.......

Start with one meaningful intention at a time, and focus on what will bring you the most joy and fulfillment.

If you are having difficulties creating what you want, it usually boils down to just a few things. The first one is not being specific with your intentions. The second is not following through with aligned actions. The third, which can take a little work, is an old program that becomes the obstacle that interferes with what you want to create. Be aware that if obstacles, and interferences get in the way of your intentions, the interference is for a reason and needs to be worked through. If you ignore the obstacles they will continue to appear and cause stress until you start to address them.

When you set your intention, act upon it. When you let go of expectations and experiences key to manifesting the intention they appear as if by magic. The fullness of being you is related to being in alignment with the flow of your creative life energy that is manifesting what you desire.

Responsibilities

Everything you think, feel, express, and create is all you! Your life will be determined by your dominant thoughts and your reactions to those thoughts. No one else can create your thoughts, no one else can feel your feelings, they are all uniquely yours every minute of every day. A paradigm shift occurs when you realize that you are the creator of how you experience your life and how your body expresses healthy or unhealthy states. Everything you are experiencing is for a reason. There are no mistakes. If you feel stuck and limited, the purpose of your experiences is to help you heal, grow, and evolve so you can enjoy your life.

Personal Responsibility

Personal responsibility is being accountable for what you think, feel, act, and taking charge of what you hold inside. Blaming others for what they feel is how people give their power away. When we blame others, we transfer responsibility to them for the way we experience life. You cannot make anyone else feel anything. What others feel is their responsibility and creation. What you feel is yours. When you intentionally take responsibility for how you feel at any given moment and let go of blame, you empower yourself. Then you can start to live your life and make empowering choices instead of reacting to old default conditioning. If everyone was responsible for how they felt and reacted, we would have so much more emotional intelligence in the world.

"You've got to know what you want. This is central to acting on your intentions. When you know what you want, you realize that all there is left then is time management. You'll manage your time to achieve your goals because you clearly know what you're trying to achieve in your life." - Patch Adams

Affirmations for Being Intentional

I set my intention with clarity, focus, and awareness.
I manifest my intention by knowing what,
why, and taking action.
I take full responsibility for everything I think,
feel, express, and create.
Having a stellar attitude gives me
positive, joyful results.

Chapter 6
Life by Design

Designing Your Life
Prioritize Your To-Do Exercise
Complete the Incompletes
Complete the Incomplete Exercise
Being Inspired
Your Attitude Matters
Make Attitude a Priority
Inner Guidance
Affirmations

Creative Flow States
Unique Concepts
Being Bold
Creating Services or Products
Affirmations

Chapter 6
Life by Design

"Decide on your most important task. Begin immediately and work on that task with self-discipline until it is 100% complete. In life, all success comes from completing tasks. It's not from working at tasks, it's from completing tasks. It is only when you complete tasks that you become successful." - Brian Tracy

Designing Your Life

Build the life you've always dreamed of by design. There are areas of life that take up more time than others, like relationships and career. None of us have the time, energy, and resources to do all the things we want. Sometimes there are constraints around the things we cannot control or change. If you have a lot of things to do and are not organized that can be overwhelming, and you may end up doing very little. It's important to spend your time and energy on what matters and align those things with your values. This is key to a more fulfilling life. Every time I prioritize my most important tasks it helps me to accomplish my aspirations and goals. When I accomplish my goals, I am energized and excited to share the results. So, fill your day with high priority tasks, and you will accomplish more, get more done in less time, and have more time for other fun stuff.

Prioritize Your To-Do Exercise

Now, prioritize your to-do list and complete the following exercise in your Inspirational Journal:

- *First, make a list of all those things to do.*
- *Second, put a circle around the most important things to do.*
- *Third, put the circled things into numbered priority order and tick them off as they are completed.*
- *Make sure that when you complete a task, you celebrate that completion.*

Complete the Incompletes

Often people get frustrated with themselves when they have incompletes. These incompletes can affect other areas of life, such as starting a new project or job that requires learning a new skill. If you keep putting off developing the new skill, you prevent your life from unfolding in a new direction. It can make you feel frustrated or depressed. Incompletes prevent you from moving forward by not accomplishing or learning a new skill. That can become an energetic obstacle that distracts you from what you want to create. Incompletes create energy leaks and distractions. When there are things lingering in the back of the mind that haven't been finished yet, it stops the flow and causes stress in the mind and body. This can become a bad habit.

Anyone can be excited by an initial plan or idea, but problems occur when we have to do the less fun stuff. Or when there is a fear of being judged or criticized. It's important to be selective about what you choose to focus your attention on. When you focus on a plan or project that is aligned with your highest values, it becomes easier to find the focus, inspiration, and energy required to finish what you start. It also helps fuel you to do the jobs that aren't fun but are necessary.

If you have incompletes in your life that are frustrating you or stopping your flow, answer the questions below.

Complete the Incomplete Exercise

Write down your answers to the following questions in your Inspirational Journal:

- *What is incomplete?*
- *Is this incomplete aligned with what I value the most?*
- *If so, what do I need to do to complete this?*
- *If not, is it time to let it go?*

Take time to complete your incompletes, you will be glad you did. Make sure to celebrate what you complete.

Be sure to look in the areas of your health, wellness, work, home, relationships, finances, taxes, legal matters, insurance, and any personal space or areas you are avoiding, etc.

If you do not have a value in any of these areas, then it's essential to link your highest values with the benefits of completing these tasks. For example: when I prioritize the things I can do for my health and wellbeing, I focus on more meaningful actions, giving me the energy to complete them. When I pay my bills on time, I don't incur penalties. I feel peace of mind and have more money to save or spend on what matters to me. When I clean up my home and office, I feel relaxed and have more space to be creative.

Being Inspired

Being inspired is activated by being connected to what turns you on the most. Inspiration comes from the things that excite you and wake you up in the morning that you can't wait to express. I believe in living a life full of inspiration and joy. When I'm inspired the most, I feel a sense of alignment throughout my whole being. Inspiration comes from inside, and when ignited, it becomes a force that pulls you towards completing your goal. Motivation on the other hand is something on the outside that pushes you to do or act in a certain way. This requires having a constant external source of motivation to keep you going. Inspiration allows you to change ordinary experiences into the extraordinary and be inspired from the inside out. Build your projects and goals around the things that inspire you the most.

Your Attitude Matters

Your attitude relates to your manner, disposition, and how you express yourself. Attitude influences an individual's choice of action, and the responses from other people. Attitude is everything. People are being hired these days for their stellar attitude above their accomplishments. It is a great advantage to have both skills and a great attitude. Attitude is a choice and it's contagious. People do not react well to a bad attitude, as it creates tension and stress that can impact you and the people around you. People do not feel safe around others with a bad attitude and will either defend themselves or retreat.

However, if you have a positive attitude, you can usually reduce or prevent stressful situations and create a safer environment for others around you. This means creating an environment that encourages people to feel trust, acceptance, and value so they can be open to expression, learning, and growing.

Make Attitude a Priority

A positive mental attitude (PMA) was a concept first presented in 1937 by Napoleon Hill in his book "Think and Grow Rich." Attitude is a priority as it determines a lot more than you think. If you are having difficulty relating to others, maybe they are having difficulty relating to your attitude. Look at the way people respond and relate to you. Look at the way you think about other people and situations in your life, this will give you clues as to how you are coming across and how you may be expressing yourself. In the areas where you have a negative attitude, you will find it difficult to connect to others. A negative attitude will repel others. People will not say anything and may just avoid you. Having a positive mental attitude towards yourself and others will change your energy, attract others that have similar outlooks, and help you to succeed in your life. Having a positive mental attitude is a choice. Make yours a priority.

Here are a few key ideas for creating an empowered positive mental attitude:
Encourage yourself every day with empowering words and language such as;

- *I am worthy, I love and accept myself, I am a creative genius.*

- *Surround yourself with inspiring people that have a good PMA — Give others who criticize, gossip, or judge a wide berth as they will drain your energy and drag you down.*
- *Make healthy choices for your life. Choose an exercise that's fun. Maintain your water intake to nourish your cells. Eat to live and sustain your health. Rejuvenate and regenerate with good consistent sleep.*
- *Mindful Meditation in the morning will set up your day with inspiration, focus, and clarity, and help you wind down to sleep peacefully at night.*
- *Be in a state of gratitude for your life. When you are in gratitude, it is hard to be negative. Gratitude is a powerful attitude.*

Inner Guidance

Inner guidance is learning to tune into your natural wisdom with awareness. When you develop inner awareness of who you are, why you do what you do, and know what you really want, you'll discover the true meaning of inspiration, contentment, and happiness. With inner awareness, any emptiness you have inside finally dissolves. This is because you fill the void by simply becoming consciously aware instead of living your life on autopilot. You also stop looking for the answers "out there" and listen with awareness from within. Your inner guidance will naturally direct you to start focusing on goals and actions that are the most fulfilling for you and others. As your life unfolds with new awareness, you are drawn towards accomplishing what you need to do in order to achieve your desired goals. You will develop deeper connections with people more easily than you ever did before.

When you allow the real you to emerge, people start to notice a new radiance and happiness about you. You will naturally want to share your joy of life with others and connect with your deeper spiritual essence. Meditation and other mindfulness practices can be an excellent way to tap into your inner guidance. Regular practice can help you to connect to your deepest inner wisdom. There have been times in my life when I didn't have a logical answer for why I made certain decisions. I learned to trust my inner guidance because it felt right for me in that moment. The biggest challenge for most of us is trusting our inner guidance. Everyone has the capacity to receive, interpret, and successfully use their inner guidance. You have this genuinely powerful ability when you tune in with awareness. To make the best choices observe your body's sensations as well as your thoughts, so you can examine what your reactions are telling you. Then ask your inner guidance, "does this align with my values, is it inspiring, and is it worth spending my precious time on?" Your whole life will, all of a sudden, look and feel completely different. Develop inner awareness and trust your own inner guidance.

"Lead a life of your own design, on your own terms. Not one that others or the environment have scripted for you." - Tony Robbins

Affirmations for Designing My Life

Inspiration is activated by being connected
to what turns me on the most.
I prioritize my most important tasks to
achieve my goals.
I choose to have a good positive mental attitude.
My good attitude will help me get what I want.
I tune into myself to make better choices.
I listen and trust my inner guidance.

Creative Flow States

"I learned that courage was not the absence of fear, but the triumph over it. The brave man is not he who does not feel afraid, but he who conquers that fear." - Nelson Mandela

We are all creators. Up until now, what you know about being creative and creating your ideas is a conglomeration of what you've learned from other people's ideas. Creating is the essence of you, your uniqueness, and what you want to express to the world. When you know yourself, and what you desire, you will be inspired to do whatever it takes to complete your aspirations. Creative limitations come from limited thinking, beliefs, and comparing your abilities with others. Limitations also come from unrealistic expectations from yourself and other people. This can lead you to doubt your abilities. The truth is we are all different. Allowing yourself to be uniquely creative is rewarding, and there is a natural flow of joy, happiness, and peace. To start your creative flow, set an intention to do so. Create an environment and a time to be creative. When you have the time and space, you will be more likely to play and have fun doing the creative stuff. When you are in a creative flow state, that means being completely present and fully absorbed in a task.

Here are a few key ways for achieving creative flow states:

- *Have a clean, clear environment.*
- *Clear away any distractions.*
- *Choose work you love to do.*
- *Focus on the most important thing first.*
- *Be inspired by what you are doing.*

- *Have fun and enjoy yourself.*
- *Let go of expectations.*
- *Take regular breaks when you have longer periods of concentration. For example, I take a mini break after 45 mins to an hour of concentrated work.*
- *Reap the rewards of completion and create more flow states.*

Unique Concepts

The most successful unique concepts are ones that provide others with an experience they'll never forget. So how do you start? Well, first, you need some inspiration. Go back and look at the answers to the questions: "*Who are you? What are your unique gifts, skills, and abilities? What do you want? What do you love to do? Why do you want that? Why is that important to you? What* would that mean if you had that?" These answers are about you. Mindful meditation states will help you tune into and allow the creative juices to flow.

Being Bold

Being bold is a mindset. It's being confident in your convictions even when others back out. When you are bold, you are going beyond what you think you are capable of and stepping up, even in the face of fear. Expressing boldness is when you stand up to speak about what you are inspired about, even when you are out of your comfort zone. This is challenging for many people, but it is outside of the comfort zone that we grow the most. It takes courage to do something different and purposeful.

Creating Services or Products

If you are wanting to produce something that you hope other people will buy or want as a service or product, it is important to look at the next level questions;

- Who are these products or services for?
- How do you want these people to feel?
- What do you want these people to experience?
- What are they going to get out of your unique product or service?

People love to buy for all sorts of reasons. If you are hoping to make money from your product or service, you need to know what those reasons are and which demographic you are targeting. In other words, who is your ideal client, and what real tangible benefits are they going to get from working with you.

The architect of the creative mind is you, and with the help of your brilliant abilities, you can design the life you really want with creative consciousness.

"The delicate balance of mentoring someone is not creating them in your own image, but giving them the opportunity to create themselves." - Steven Spielberg

Affirmations for Creative Flow States

I create the states I want to experience.
Being creative is a fun opportunity
to express myself.
I create from my unique essence.
Every day is a new opportunity to
create something new.
I am a creative genius, and I express my inspiration.
I make time and space for creative flow states.

Chapter 7
Making Changes

The Art of Letting Go
Affirmations
Physical Release
Conscious Breathing
Conscious Breathing Exercise
Empowering Affirmations
Self-Empowering Affirmations
Attitude of Gratitude
Gratitude Exercise
Breakthrough Tapping
How Tapping Works
Tapping Points
What to Say When Tapping
How to Aim When Tapping
State Anchors
Making a shift
Changing Your Mental and Emotional States
Affirmations
Creating a Vision for Your Life
Life Vision Exercise
Your Vision
Your Vision Exercise
Creating a Ripple Effect
Affirmations
Creating Empowered States Daily
Learn to Observe Your Thoughts
Gratitude is an Attitude
Continuous Learning
Personal Empowerment Tools
Resources

Chapter 7
Making Changes

"Nothing in the universe can stop you from letting go and starting over." - Guy Finley

The Art of Letting Go

Every moment is a chance to let go and feel peaceful. Some people hold onto problems however. They become conditioned and these problems become very familiar, and it gives them a sense of identity. Being attached to problems can be so deeply ingrained into the fiber of our being that they seem almost impossible to let go of. When we identify in this way, we produce stress in the mind and body, create health issues, and accept this state as normal. Clinging to familiar conditioned patterns in the mind is extremely energy draining.

Letting go can be one of the most difficult lessons to learn in life, whether it's letting go of feelings like guilt, anger, resentment, love, loss, or betrayal. If we are holding on to these familiar feelings and emotions, change is never easy. Some people fight to hold on to how they feel, and at the same time, they fight to let go. Letting go is how you release what no longer serves you.

The concept of letting go means accepting the things you cannot change and doing something about the things you can. In other words, letting go is a choice to decide that you will no longer ruminate on things that are out of your control and focus on what you can control. It is accepting that whatever happened in the past is now over. Those moments from the past only exist in the distorted memory banks of the mind. This means we distort and delete past memories based on our beliefs and our perceptual version of reality. The human memory is extremely unreliable, especially when it comes to details. It is impossible to remember every little detail we experience so our brain fills in the gaps with other memories and imagination to build what we think and believe is a complete picture. Research shows that we cannot trust our memories no matter how good we think we remember a situation or event. It has been discovered that by using suggestions and asking persuading questions, an eyewitness to an event can produce detailed memories that are completely false. These memories feel just as real and accurate to the witness as what happened in the actual event.

Past memories that you ruminate on create bad feelings and emotions, keeping you imprisoned in self-destructive patterns that can affect every area of your life. It's difficult to make a new life or immerse yourself in a new relationship or career when you are holding onto the emotional ties from the last one. It's important to realize that you will find it hard to move forward unless you learn to let go, forgive yourself, and release past hurts. The sooner we let go of our past hurts, the sooner we release ourselves from the patterns that hurt us. By resenting the past, we hold onto the past and we cannot heal. With all that being said, there is one fundamental aspect to letting go and that is, you must want change to get change.

One of the reasons for holding onto past hurts is because they are incomplete. For example, sometimes we feel resentment, bitterness, and injustice for what was done, and we want others to pay. Other times it is because there is some benefit or secondary gain to holding onto that problem. When we benefit from our problem there is an indirect advantage. For instance, if we don't do what others want, they withhold love, money, or some other perceived value. We keep the problem to get the benefit. Many people hang on to past trauma, pain, and hurt to try to protect themselves from being hurt again in the future. The problem with that is that they have to keep the problems, pain, and reactivity inside themselves. This attracts more of what they are trying to avoid.

Often problems that occurred in childhood that were unresolved can affect a person's whole life until there is a resolution, or when they can let go of the problem. It's important to heal the past's hurts and overcome the pain that is felt in the present. This can happen easily when we allow ourselves the opportunity to let go and feel that it's safe to do so. When resolving the incompletes there is growth, a sense of peace, and learning from the past that brings wisdom and healing.

The real secret to letting go is allowing and being. The tapping process I share later in this chapter is a powerful way of letting go of any deep-seated issues that may be holding you back in your life. The magnificent journey of today can only begin when we learn to let go of the things that bother us from the past.

> *"In the process of letting go, you will lose many things from the past, but you will find yourself."* - Deepak Chopra

Affirmations for Letting Go

Letting go is easy because I make it easy.
It is safe to let go of what no longer serves me.
I let go of what is out of my control and
focus on what I can control.
I let go of the past because it's over.
I let go of stress and breathe.
I easily let go of stress.

Physical Release

"The implication is that this basic idea we have that we are controlled by our genes is false. It's an idea that turns us into victims. I'm saying we are the creators of our situation. The genes are merely the blueprints. We are the contractors, and we can adjust those blueprints. And we can even rewrite them." - Bruce Lipton

Sometimes there is a need for the body to have a physical release. Stress symptoms can affect your physical and emotional health. Stress is expressed in the body in a number of ways. Such as; muscle tension in the shoulders, stiffness in the neck, aching back, upset stomach, and tension headaches. When you are stressed the muscles in the body tighten. Prolonged stress can create long term physical problems that can affect your emotional health if not addressed. Your body is always communicating and giving you feedback. Physical symptoms and illness expressed in the body often begin from emotional and mental states. Physical release occurs when stress and tension are dissolved in the body and mind. Breakthrough Tapping is a great way to release long-held stress in the body and create a calm state of mind very quickly.

Conscious Breathing

Conscious breathing is a powerful way to release stress and tension from the mind and body. A simple way to breathe more consciously is to focus your attention on the flow of air going in and out of your nose. You can try it for yourself by closing your eyes and observing the cool air flowing into your nasal passage and lungs, and then noticing the warmer air flowing out again. Do this for five to ten minutes with awareness, and you will notice a considerable change in how you think and feel. This is one of the easiest ways to bring yourself back into the present moment and release stress. It only takes a short amount of time to do. Of course, to get the most from conscious breathing it needs to be practiced regularly. Conscious breathwork becomes an excellent natural tool that you can use to help you feel calm and centered when you need to release stress. By incorporating focused breath and movement together, you can quickly bring about a powerful sense of calm and peace within the mind and body system. Clear your mind and calm your body with a few minutes of conscious breathing.

> "When the breath wanders the mind also is unsteady. But when the breath is calmed the mind too will be still, and the yogi achieves long life. Therefore, one should learn to control the breath." - Yogi Swatmarama, Hatha Yoga Pradipika

Conscious Breathing Exercise

A simple way to become centered and
calm is to focus on your breath.
Sit in a relaxed position with your body
lengthened and close your eyes.
Start by taking three deep belly breaths. Slowly
inhale through your nose and exhale
through your mouth.
Then focus on your natural breath for ten breaths.
Now inhale through your nose and exhale
slowly through pursed lips.
Continue this process for five minutes. Observe
the air flowing in and slowly out
through your pursed lips.

Empowering Affirmations

Affirmations are words we use to affirm what we believe and change how we feel. We tend to think of affirmations as being of a positive nature but often, it is the negative words that can be our biggest and most powerful affirmations.

Negative affirmations keep us in alignment with negative thoughts that we believe about ourselves. When we change what we are saying to ourselves we begin to change what we hold inside. Your words are powerful and determine what you hold inside, so choose what you affirm wisely. You can use empowering affirmations any time and also use them with the tapping process. Here are some to get you started.

Self-Empowering Affirmations

Right now, as I am; I totally love and accept myself.
It is safe to change the way I feel.
I create new opportunities.
I live in the present moment.
I am my own best friend.
It is safe to stand in my own power.
I am cool, calm, and relaxed.
I take responsibility for my actions,
feeling and emotions.
I am a healing machine.
I see myself through loving eyes.
I am kind, warm, and loving to myself.
Today I choose to act in my own best interest.

Attitude of Gratitude

An attitude of gratitude is a powerful state. Being in a state of gratitude changes the expression of your body's DNA by turning on healthy gene cells and switching off unhealthy gene cells. When you are in the state of gratitude, you change the cellular messages in your body. If you can change your cellular messages you can overcome illness and keep your body in balance. When you express gratitude, you change the vibration and chemistry in your body. Practicing an attitude of gratitude can literally change the way your body reacts and responds. In this way you can feel healthier, be happier, have better relationships, and increase your productivity. Gratitude is the quality of being thankful and the ability to show appreciation for kindness expressed.

"As we express our gratitude, we must never forget that the highest appreciation is not to utter words, but to live by them." - John F. Kennedy

Think about what you are grateful for. If you can see an image in your mind, it helps. If you are unable to see an image in your mind, you can write it down. When you are grateful practice really feeling it and feel it through every fiber of your being. Practice states of being in gratitude often. When you are in gratitude, you are in the present moment.

Gratitude Exercise

Answer the following questions and write them down in your Inspirational Journal:

- What are you grateful for today?
- What relationships are you grateful for?

- What is a hard lesson that you were grateful to learn?
- What have others done in your life that you are grateful for?
- What quality of your physical health do you feel grateful for?
- What aspect of your personality are you grateful for?
- What one thing have you enjoyed about doing your job lately?
- What made you laugh or smile today?

Practicing gratitude can help you manage stress better and increase feelings of happiness and well-being. Keeping a journal of gratitude is a fabulous way to find inspiration when you need it. When you read your journal, it will trigger your memories and get inspirational ideas flowing.

Embracing a grateful attitude can influence almost every aspect of your life in a powerful way, including your relationships, mood, job satisfaction, health, etc.

Breakthrough Tapping

"A positive state of mind is not merely good for you, it benefits everyone with whom you come in to contact, literally changing the world." - Dalai Lama

What is Breakthrough Tapping? Breakthrough Tapping is among the most powerful personal development tools to heal and release the obstacles that get in the way of living the best life. Breakthrough Tapping is also one of the most effective treatment methods for addressing and resolving mental, emotional, and stress-related challenges. The premise with tapping is that no matter what challenges are occurring in your life, there is a correlating unresolved and incomplete emotional issue that is expressing itself. The process of tapping can profoundly lower harmful stress levels. The points we tap on directly correspond to the body's fight or flight response system. Tapping stimulates change in the brain, called neuroplasticity, making it easy to let go of unproductive subconscious patterns and programs to bring your mind and body into balance. This process is how you get out of your own way!

How Tapping Works

Tapping works with the mind and body by interrupting and breaking through conditioned mental and emotional patterns, states, and reactions. When tapping, the intent is to focus on releasing and clearing unproductive memories, ideas, beliefs, conditioning, and emotional reactions. Breakthrough Tapping can also address the underlying ways that people produce anxiety, depression, PTSD, and trauma. Tapping is a more permanent solution than standard treatments, as we aim specifically at the cause of the problem to release stress and emotions. As a result, this process helps recondition the central nervous system to reduce and eliminate harmful stress and the chemical effects in the body. Breakthrough Tapping opens new options to create productive receptive states to make positive change. The natural process of tapping quickly brings about equilibrium to the whole mind-body system. What we want to do is tap into your mind's own ability to heal.

Tapping Points

When tapping, one of the first skills to develop is how to let things go. Letting go is a natural process. You don't need to "do" anything except let go of the limiting things the brain is conditioned to hang on to. Your success depends on allowing yourself to let go of what no longer serves you. We use the 5 Faster EFT/Eutaptics points that summarize the original 15 EFT acupuncture/acupressure points in this sequence. The five main tapping points we use are (1) in-between the eyes, (2) on the side of the eyes, (3) under the eyes, (4) under the collarbone, and then (5) hold onto the wrist. We finish each round by holding onto the wrist and creating an anchor for connecting to a peaceful state of mind.

In addition, the physical act of tapping relates to specific parts of the body that we tap on, known as meridian acupuncture points. These points correlate to particular organs in the body and act to stimulate the central nervous system to bring about relaxation in the body. Tapping can also be seen as a process to focus the mind while letting go of painful states in the mind. When you tap on the pressure points, you are opening a communication channel between the mind and body and shifting perception simultaneously. The focus is on breaking up the signals between the mental patterns in the mind, and the emotions felt in the body. In other words, you are sending a signal to the body that "turns on" self-regulatory mechanisms while disrupting in old patterns that produce a release of energy and a shift in perception. Above all, this tapping process allows you to experience quick and lasting changes in the way your mind thinks about your problems. Tapping is a powerful alternative treatment to get relief from physical pain and emotional stress. Once you let go of what is holding you back, you can also use the tapping process to focus your mind on more meaningful thoughts and activities.

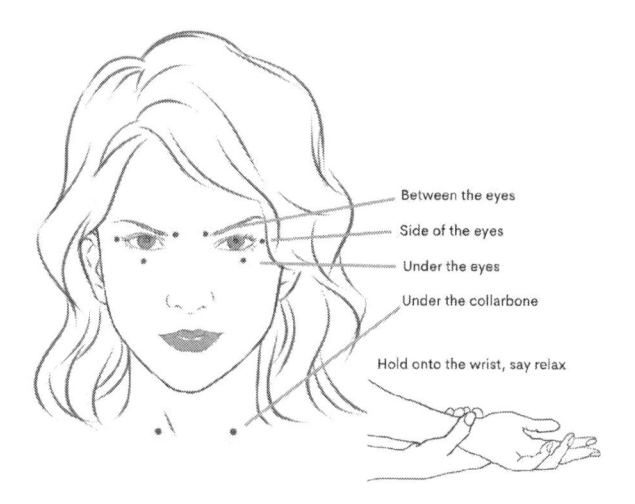

- Between the eyes
- Side of the eyes
- Under the eyes
- Under the collarbone
- Hold onto the wrist, say relax

What to Say When You Tap

Here are some statements that you can use to let go of things you don't want when you are ready for change. Repeat as necessary.

- "I let it go."
- "I choose to let it go."
- "It's easy to let it go."
- "It's time to let it go."
- "I'm okay to let it go."
- "It's safe to let it go."
- "I release and let it go."
- "I just let it go."

How to Aim When Tapping

The important thing with aiming is paying attention to what you are doing in your mind. The first thing you do is to notice how you know, and second, let it go. When you notice how you know, these are the internal references. This means when you are bothered about something, you notice a physical sensation in your body, a feeling like tension in the stomach, tightness in the shoulders, pain in the chest, or a headache. It could be from a memory, and you notice an image going on inside your mind from a past experience that bothers you. Once you "notice how you know", what's going on inside, that's when you tap, release, and let it go. You keep aiming at the problem and tapping until it has changed and you feel different.

Be aware of any resistance, triggers, or old programs that may be keeping you stuck and halting the process of change. These are things to pay attention to and let go of. If there is any resistance such as when you say to yourself, "I'm scared to let this go," this means there may be some value or benefit to holding on to what you have within. The strong emotional attachment to the problem is something you want to become aware of so you can let go of all those little aspects and set yourself free.

State Anchor

A round of tapping is finished after you tap on each place several times and end up holding your wrist. At the end of each round of tapping, you will take a deep breath in and anchor yourself in a state of peace. Taking a deep breath is an essential part of the process. The breath is directly connected to the central nervous system, autonomic nervous system and stimulates a parasympathetic nervous system response. How we breathe affects how we think and feel. When we take a deep breath in, we tell our autonomic nervous system that it is okay to let go of the stress now. Taking a deep breath is sending a signal to the body to go back into a relaxed state. When you want to set a positive anchor think about a happy memory, a happy time, or a memory of being in nature like the mountains, the beach, or something that makes you feel amazing, smile, or laugh.

Sometimes people find it hard to be happy because they get very good at feeling sad and unhappy. If you find it hard to find something happy, think about me supporting you right here and now. I think you're wonderful for learning how to improve your life, and I know how challenging it can be. Know that I am supporting you. During this part of the process, what you're actually doing is taking your mind to a different place. The more you do it, the stronger this anchor becomes.

Making a shift

A shift in the mind occurs when there is aimed focus. This means you use your mind to aim precisely at the internal references held in the mind. These internal references include thoughts, images, feelings, beliefs, and painful memories. Each round of tapping helps to methodically release the expression of pain and the internal references that you hold inside. As the mind lets go of these internal references, the body responds differently, allowing tension to soften and dissipate. Persistence is the key to releasing physical and emotional pain. You don't stop after trying it one time, you keep going until you feel different and have no emotional reaction to the problem. When we release stress, we start to see things in a different way. The shift occurs with a realization based on new information that changes perception. It is essential to follow through by regularly conditioning yourself to a more empowered state of being.

The tapping process helps you be present in the moment and release the resulting emotions and feelings from past events that get bottled up inside and change the thoughts and perceptions around the issues that are familiar. The results are powerful and can awaken you to a new perspective and a newly empowered state of mind. This process changes your reality and how you see yourself and the situation.

Changing Your Mental and Emotional States

*"Intelligence is the ability to
adapt to change." - Stephen Hawking*

As you can see, by doing this process, you can change your mental and emotional states and rewire your brain. When you are tapping you are changing brain plasticity. According to scientists, these changes range from individual neurons making new connections to systematic adjustments like cortical remapping. Changes can start to happen quickly when we begin to understand how neural pathways are created in the brain. When we repeatedly send the same message down a nerve cell pathway, we reinforce the pathway, and that message becomes wired in the brain. For example, if we have the same thoughts, make the same choices, and have the same attitudes and behaviors, then we create the same emotional reactions and experiences. When we decide to have different thoughts, attitudes, and behaviors, we create a completely different result. People have the ability and can build new neural pathways, not only with new behaviors but through our own imagination. Imagine and practice the new thoughts and behaviors you want over and over again. When you keep repeating and visualizing new ideas in the mind, you feel it in the body, and you literally begin to build new pathways. This new focus of your mind will retrain your brain and build emotional intelligence. Emotional intelligence provides a platform for releasing stress, self-regulation, and trusting one's own ability. You can learn to control or release disruptive impulses and knee-jerk reactions to any given situation. When we practice emotional intelligence, it connects us to our higher self so we can attain more happiness and fulfillment. We can gain a sense of purpose and liberation that was once thought of as impossible to achieve.

A group of concentrated tapping rounds is called a session. Once you feel a sense of peace after your tapping session, be in gratitude. Gratitude comes when you make peace with yourself, your challenges, and the people in your life. Gratitude flows when you are thankful for your life and experiences, and you can say, "Thank you, I love you". The state of gratitude works at a deep subconscious level and is a wonderful healing tool to round off the end of a tapping session. If there is any resentment or resistance, it is essential to continue your inner work. If you are having difficulty releasing a problem, make sure to reach out for help. Sometimes it is difficult to release deep-seated issues because of a lack of awareness of what is buried deep within our subconscious mind. Transformation is easy if you allow yourself to change. It is ultimately up to you, but know that it is always possible. You can create new brain pathways whenever you are ready to make a shift. When you are in the mindset of "I can change whatever I want", then you are sitting in the driver's seat of your life, and you get to design your life the way you have always wanted.

"One can choose to go back toward safety or forward toward growth. Growth must be chosen again and again; fear must be overcome again and again." - Abraham Maslow

Affirmations for Making Changes

I am ready to make empowering changes.
I face my challenges with strength and know
I can get through it.
I embrace the changes in my life with
curiosity and gratitude.
I am grateful for new challenges and experiences
that help me to grow and be stronger.
I am strong, courageous, and worthy of all good
things that come my way.
Having a stellar attitude gives me
positive, joyful results.
I intend to live this day to the fullest.

Creating a Vision for Your Life

"The only thing worse than being blind is having sight but no vision." - Helen Keller

Now you have learned the tools to clear the way forward. It is time to put what you have learned into practice, complete your incompletes, and let go of unresourceful states. It is not enough to just know these things. Using these tools will clear your mind and make space for more meaningful and important activities.

When your mind is clear from energy draining attachments and distractions, you can create an empowering vision for your life.

The future you want is determined by what you do right now. The life you are living today is the result of what you have done in the past, up until now, whether it was by design or default. What you have now is the manifestation of what you have done. If you want things to be different, you need to do things differently, or you will produce more of the same results.

What you do today will create your future. Consciously design the life you want to create for tomorrow, right now. This means you can decide on the goals and the vision you want for your life. There are no rules or regulations. What matters is making a decision and taking the time to sit down and work through this part. This will open your mind to new possibilities. Look at areas where you want to set new goals. Here are some areas that you may want to consider to make changes, your career, environment, finances, relationships, mind-body health, spirituality, time for meaningful activities, social, exercise, personal growth, etc.

Life Vision Exercise

Take a deep breath in, feel what it is you want to improve. Just look at one of these areas to begin. Allow your answers to come from your true and higher self.

Ask yourself:

- *What do I want in my life?*
- *How do I really want my life to be?*
- *Why do I want this to happen?*

Write your answers in your journal.

Your Vision

A vision is what you want to create in your life. Your vision is a work in progress that may develop over a number of years. A vision guides your life and provides the direction necessary to map the course of your days and the choices and decisions you make along the way. Think of the vision you create as the light that illuminates your life path.

When you tap into a vision greater than yourself, it moves and excites you. It's not about knowing how you will achieve it. It's about knowing why you want that vision for yourself and your life. When you are no longer operating from a place of fear or limitation, you can express your vision. Think of when you were a child when there were no limits to what you could do or accomplish. You just dreamed of all the things you could become when you grew up, without a thought of how you were going to do it. It's important to have something inspiring and meaningful that you are moving toward. Your vision propels your purpose. Your purpose gives your life meaning, and fulfillment. It also gives you the reasons why you do what you need to do. When you are inspired by purpose, you know how that benefits you and the people you are serving. Remember, it is not what you get from life that fulfills you, it is what you give and the value you contribute. Your vision, purpose, goals, and actions embody every area of your life. In creating your vision, it may be 2, 5, or 10 years out. Get into a positive state of being. Put yourself into a childlike state and imagine yourself limitless and open with a learner's mindset. Take the time to create a vision that inspires you. Imagine anything is possible. Create from a mindset where there are no limitations and nothing holding you back.

Your Vision Exercise

Start by asking yourself these questions that relate to your vision.

- *What is my vision?*
- *Why do I want this vision for my life?*
- *What good things might happen if I follow through with my vision?*
- *How would things be different if my vision comes true?*

Keep writing down all your answers.

Align your vision with the essence of your values. Then focus empowering thoughts on your vision, feel it in your heart, and allow yourself to submerge in this vision. Vision boards are another visual aid to help you feel inspired with energy. You will get fired up and inspired to keep going. Create a visual stimulus of what you would like to focus upon and add pictures of your goals and dreams. It will help you to aim at and attract what you want in your life. Use images and power words. Look at your vision board daily and see yourself already having those wonderful things. Imagine it and feel it. Having a meaningful vision is the fuel that you need to achieve your goals.

Creating a Ripple Effect

The ripple effect is a metaphor to help us understand cause and affect relationships between things. This means that every small change that takes place effects things around it that spread and produce other effects and eventually results in a changing world.

When I first started working as a mind-body practitioner, I didn't understand how profound the ripple effect was until I experienced it firsthand. There was a time when I wasn't sure how effective I was with my clients. One lady I worked with had severe anxiety that affected much of her life to the point that she stopped going to work and became very isolated. After a few sessions, she said she felt better, but I didn't see her again for months. Then one day, I bumped into her at the shops. She told me, with great excitement, that her whole world had changed since working with me. She went on to tell me that she finally found the courage to start doing the work she always wanted to do and was loving it. She also met a lovely man that had a wonderful family who invited her for Christmas. She then said, with tears in her eyes, that she'd had the best Christmas of her entire life. This experience taught me not to underestimate the impact or effect you might have on someone else's life when you do good work that aligns with your purpose.

Research has shown that acts of kindness can have a ripple effect that keeps going and expanding beyond what we know. When you live your life in alignment with your inspired purpose, you are producing a powerful ripple effect that goes far beyond your awareness. It is a flow of energy in motion. One thing is for sure, you are always going to create a ripple. What kind of ripple are you going to create? As the creator of your experience, you are given the power to choose what kind of ripple you will start. It is with this awareness in the present moment that you connect to your higher self, which is where your power is. You get to choose what kind of ripple you want to send out into the world starting from right now.

"You are a great being who has been given a tremendous opportunity to explore beyond yourself. The whole process is very exciting, and you will have good times and bad times. All sorts of things will happen. That's the fun of the journey." - Michael Singer

Affirmations for Creating A Vision

I have the freedom and power to
create a life I love.
My possibilities are limitless.
I am worthy and deserving of my dreams.
I am deeply fulfilled by what I love to do.
I create a vision that expresses the
love I have inside.

Creating Empowered States Daily

Here are a few key actions that will help you to start producing creative, productive, and empowered states daily.

- Before you get out of bed, take a few minutes to set your intention for the day.
- Start your day as you mean to go on.
- Stretch your body in all six directions, side to side, forward and backward, and twisting to each side.
- Write in your inspirational journal what your intention is for the day and one action that will make the biggest difference. This intentional action will propel you forward with the necessary firsts step in the right direction. This is a great practice, especially for those who want to make empowering changes.
- Practice your affirmations at the bathroom mirror. If you find this difficult to do, realize that this powerful process can reveal what might need to be addressed. Release away any negative feelings or emotions. Practice your most powerful daily affirmations to reaffirm your empowering states.

Learn to Observe Your Thoughts

- Watch your thoughts. The quality of your thoughts affects your life. Be kind to yourself.
- It is impossible to create empowering change if you are still thinking negatively.
- You get in your life what you think about most. (Thoughts are that powerful.)
- Dissolve your negative thoughts, feelings, highly charged emotional memories, and limiting beliefs that do not serve you now. Use the tapping process to help you do this. Retrain your mind to have a positive mental attitude about yourself and your life.
- Make sure that your thoughts, words, and actions are aligned with what you value the most. This will help you experience joyful, inspiring, and fulfilling states.
- By observing your thoughts and feelings without attachment will naturally quieten your mind and bring about a state of inner peace.

Gratitude is an Attitude

- Simply stating or writing daily what you are grateful for sets a positive tone and attracts more of these things into your life. When I started doing this, I would write out three things I was grateful for on a daily basis. Then I feel it in my body as I read them out loud.
- Having an "Attitude of Gratitude" for what you have right now brings you back into the present moment.
- When addressing negative emotions, thank them for revealing themselves. Feel the emotions and then let them go. Negative

emotions are there because something needs to be expressed and addressed. They are a healing opportunity.

Continuous Learning

- Your brain has an amazing capacity for continuous and perpetual learning.
- Inspirational Journaling is a way to express yourself and rewire your brain. Writing by hand helps make your writing a more holistic activity activating more learning centers of the brain.
- If you stop learning, your mental muscle practices old conditioned patterns. The brain creates new neuropathways when we continue learning new information.
- Reading something new and inspirational will open your mind to new possibilities and create inspiring ideas.
- Sign up for an activity that you've always wanted to do and challenge yourself. Get out of your comfort zone. Remember, it's always up to you to keep yourself challenged in a way that empowers and inspires you! No one else will do it for you.

Personal Empowerment Tools

- Breakthrough Tapping — Dissolve the emotions, limitations, and barriers that distract you from living the life you want to create. Use this process for creating deep changes and empowering states of mind.

- Conscious Breathing — It only takes a few minutes to connect with your breath to bring you back in the powerful present moment.
- Journaling — Read your journal to create inspiring states.
- Vision boards - Create a visual stimulus of what you would like to bring about. Add pictures of your goals and dreams. Your vision board will help you aim, focus, and manifest what you want in your life. Use images and power words and look at your vision board daily. See yourself feeling wonderful and having those things as a reflection of what you feel inside. Imagine and feel it. In manifesting what you want, it always starts with loving yourself and feeling good within, so you automatically attract good things outside.
- Affirmations — Practice empowering affirmations to change your mental state.
- Meditation — Practicing the quality of being calm and absent of thought for 15 minutes a day can put you in touch with your core self and inner peace.
- Relaxation — Rejuvenate, regenerate, and nourish your whole mind and body all the way down to the cellular level.
- Time for Nurture — Make time for your precious self. You are treating yourself in loving ways. Take a soak in a hot bath using oils, body lotion, or whatever feels good. Take time to read an inspirational book. Say empowering affirmations and be present and aware.
- Mindset Programs — Listen to inspirational teachings to change unconscious programs and support empowering attitudes.

"One of the most satisfying events of being human is the experience of becoming the person you were meant to become." - Kim Ryder

Conclusion

You are here for a reason...to live your life
purposefully and reach your full potential...from
everything that you are to everything that you are
capable of being...and share your
glorious gifts with the world.

Refuse to let anything stand in the
way of living your dreams.
Allow yourself to shine and illuminate your life!

Resources

Our website has free health and wellness resources to support your empowering journey. Here you will find special audio recordings and videos, plus other inspirational programs and courses to support your personal growth and continued learning.

https://www.totalintegratedtherapy.com/resources-for-health-and-wellness/

For other video, resources head to our YouTube channel "Breakthrough Mindsets"
https://www.youtube.com/breakthroughmindsets/

About the Author

Kim Ryder is a heart-centered teacher, mind-body specialist, Breakthrough Tapping practitioner, Integral Hatha Yoga instructor, and published author. Dedicated to helping people release limiting beliefs and align their lives to take inspired action and create the life they truly want. Kim has a background in tapping therapy, remedial massage, and over 25 years' experience teaching Integral Hatha Yoga. She has lived and worked in Australia, the United Kingdom, and now in the United States, sharing her knowledge through personal one-on-one consulting sessions, regular workshops, and seminars. Kim's unique approach helps her clients learn how to relax, feel happy, confident, and empowered.

Kim started practicing yoga over twenty-five years ago as a young mother wanting to improve her health and wellbeing. After many years of attending regular yoga classes and her own self-practice, she wanted to do more to help others.

In 1993 Kim attained her remedial massage therapy certification and trained to become a teacher with the British Wheel of Yoga in the UK in 1995. She studied for three years under the guidance of Swami Satchidananda Ma. During the first year of teacher training, she began teaching small groups of students. She then taught at several adult education centers around Southwest England and began conducting her own regular classes in Berkshire.

In 2002 she moved back to Australia, where she grew up and went back to college to attain a diversional therapy leisure and lifestyle certification. During this time, Kim built a successful yoga studio in Adelaide Hills, South Australia. She began teaching regular Integral Hatha Yoga classes, meditation groups, and workshops for women's health and wellness. Kim then began integrating various in-depth healing disciplines, techniques, and modalities to help students and clients heal and connect authentically.

In 2013 Jeff Nash, director of Habilitat, invited Kim to participate as a volunteer for a two-week tapping healing marathon at Habilitat in Hawaii, a long-term drug and alcohol rehabilitation center with over 120 residents. One of her highlights was teaching early morning yoga classes to residents and staff. They embraced Kim's yoga and enjoyed all aspects of the practice. During this visit, Kim met her future husband, David Ryder, who also got invited for his tapping and mind-body skills. Kim and David soon discovered they were a powerful healing team when they combined their skills to help their clients.

In 2014 Kim made the big move to the United States to be with David and begin a new direction, sharing their unique and powerful work. Kim and David ran a successful wellness clinic in Dallas, Texas. Much of their local work was based on word of mouth and referrals from both pain clinics and psychologists for their unique and effective healing style. They also traveled regularly through the US, Canada, and Australia teaching workshops.

In 2016 they moved their business Total Integrated Therapy to Canby, Oregon. They offer regular mind-body workshops, online training, and one-on-one sessions for individuals to reach their personal and professional goals. Kim and Dave continue to share their wealth of knowledge with groups and individuals, locally in their Oregon clinic, internationally, and online, to help their clients break through physical pain and emotional stress to achieve new empowering states of mind.

For more information about Kim or to attend a training workshop, seminar, or to work with her in person, please contact:

E-mail: info@totalintegratedtherapy.com
Website: www.totalintegratedtherapy.com
Phone: (503) 862 8573

Literature Cited and Additional Good References:

Autobiography of a yogi – 1946 - The Law of Success Paramahansa Yogananda
Hatha Yoga Pradipika – Light on Hatha Yoga, Swami Muktibodhananda Saraswati 1998
The Secret Language of The Body - Inna Segal 2007
Long Walk to Freedom - The Autobiography of Nelson Mandela 1994
Earthly Paradise - William Morris, 1834 – 1896
A New Earth - By Eckhart Tolle 2005
The Biology of Belief – Unleashing the Power of Consciousness, Matter, and Miracles. Lipton, Bruce, Ph.D. 2005
Molecules of Emotion – The Science Behind Mind-Body Medicine. Pert, Candace B., Ph.D.1997
Heal Your Body – Louise L. Hay 2009
The Courage to Heal – Ellen Bass and Laura Davis 2008
Handbook to Higher Consciousness - Ken Keyes, JR. 1994
The Bhagavad Gita - Translated by Juan Mascaro 2003
The Breakthrough Experience – John Demartini 2016
I Can Change the Way I Feel – Tap Away Your Troubles – Kim Ryder 2014

Printed in Great Britain
by Amazon